Children and Painting

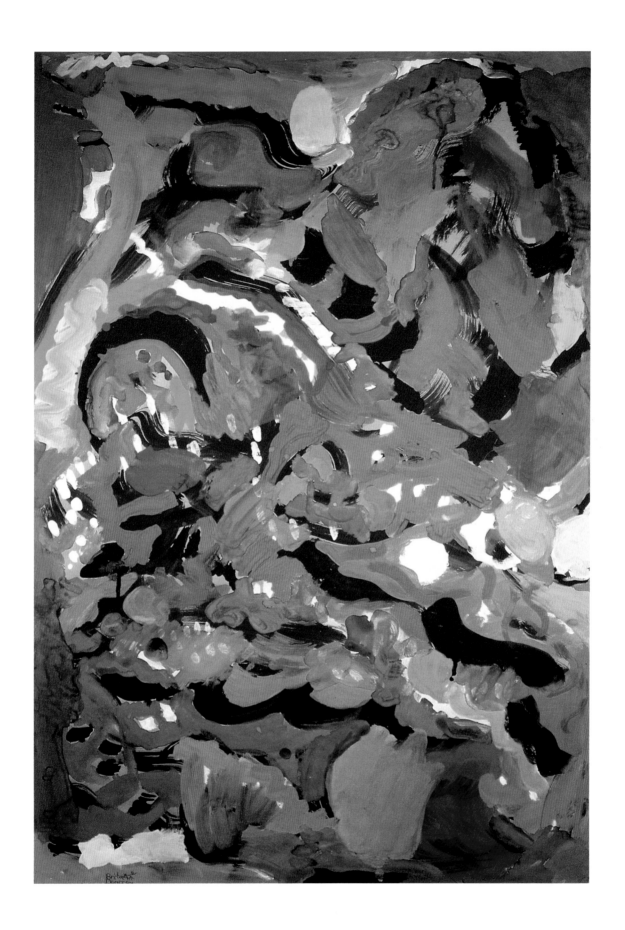

Children and Painting

Cathy Weisman Topal

Davis Publications, Inc.   **Worcester, Massachusetts**

For my parents, Charna and Philip Weisman, who fostered my love of learning and of art.

Acknowledgments
The content of this book is the outgrowth of watching, interacting with and listening to children. During the past twenty years of teaching art I feel grateful for the many children who have enriched my life and shown me their unique ways of looking at the world and of working with paint. Many of their paintings enliven the pages of this book as they tell different parts of the story. Unless otherwise noted, all paintings by children were done by students at Fort Hill Preschool and the Smith College Campus School.

My deepest appreciation goes to Diane Harr, with whom I share an art teaching position. She has been my partner in learning. Many of the organizational tips and activities come from lessons that Diane developed — especially ocean painting, mixed media color collage, Native American portraits, Colonial portraits, Cubist portraits, Fauvist trees and autumn grasses.

Lella Gandini's research gave me a way to begin looking at the paintings of pre-school children. Sheila Kelly contributed to my understanding of how children learn. Jan Szymaszek, Janice Henderson and Sheila have worked with me in presenting more than one strategy for solving a problem when working with a group of children. Shauneen Kroll spent endless afternoons with me, pointing out subtle stages of growth that I would otherwise have missed. Sally Bagg and Gretchen Burdick were consultants for the section on music. Polly Anderson McCusker from the Buckland-Shelburne School, and Jaclyn Coe, Barry McCormack, Susan Routhier and Laurie Stowell from the schools in Northampton, Massachusetts, also contributed slides of children's artwork.

Many of my art education students at Smith College have helped with sections of the book. Karen Melcher and Amelia Hayes worked on stormy weather and value paintings. Laurel Loomis developed parts of the chapter on watercolor. Susan Thompson worked out part of the lesson on dragons. The section on "Me and a Special Adult" was an outgrowth of Shalla Junejo's student teaching project.

The chapter on black ink paintings was a special challenge. Professor Daniel Gardner clarified my understanding of black ink painting traditions. Yoon Park showed me that each subtle brush variation has meaning. The beautiful illustrations in this section were painted by Belinda Zucker and Dora Chen.

I am happy to be able to share several photographs of children's paintings from the early childhood schools in the city of Reggio Emilia, Italy. I thank the teachers for giving me permission to include these paintings.

The Smith College Campus School and the Department of Education and Child Study have been extremely supportive of my work on this project, which has been ongoing for the past five years. Special thanks go to Chris Barbuto, who typed many letters. I am grateful to the Smith College Museum of Art for a great many of the fine art examples in the book. My thanks also go to the many painters who have given me permission to use their paintings.

Martha Siegel, Wyatt Wade and Claire Golding at Davis Publications, Inc. made working on this project fun — most of the time.

My three wonderful daughters, Simone, Rachel and Claire, helped by trying out activities, posing for photographs and working on illustrations. My husband, Sam, has been my most enthusiastic and understanding companion throughout this long process.

All photographs of student artwork provided by Diane Harr or Cathy Weisman Topal, unless otherwise noted.

Cover: *Flowers* (detail), Alex Batten, grade 5.
Cover inset: *A Group of Kids*, Justine Beauvais, grade 3.
Back cover: *Flowers*, Alex Batten, grade 5.
Half title page: Hannah Scaife, grade 3.
Frontispiece: *Wild Carnival*, Brita Dempsey, grade 5.

Design: Susan Marsh

Library of Congress Catalog Card Number: 91-073902
ISBN: 87192-241-X
10 9 8 7 6

Contents

Devon Ducharme, grade 1.

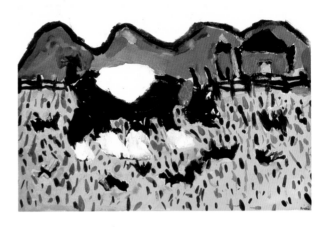

Kristin Davies, grade 3.

Columbine, Ann Rundquist, grade 4.

Family Portrait, Samantha Sacks, grade 1.

Emily Montgomery, age 4.

Introduction

The activities in this book are designed to draw children into the dynamic, interactive, ever–changing process that is the essence of painting. Each activity presents an open-ended point from which a painting can grow. The aim of this book is to break concepts down to their simplest levels and encourage students to work with one particular concept and technique at a time. Once children understand a basic concept and have experienced a new technique, teachers can easily suggest additional challenges.

All the activities are appropriate for children in kindergarten and any of the other elementary grades. Many of the activities in Part One are appropriate for preschool children. When children of different ages approach the same subject or activity, what varies is the number of steps and amount of time needed to understand the concept and practice the skill. The amount of control and sophistication used in developing an idea varies as well. Though this book is geared toward working with children, it is actually a basic painting textbook for any beginning painter. Basics are the same whether a person is six or eighty-six!

How Children Develop in Painting

In order to guide students as they paint, it is important to be aware that children go through fairly predictable stages as they develop abilities to use paint to express themselves. It is by watching and interacting with a group of children that a teacher picks up on the group's interests and selects a place to begin.

Children as young as two years old can make a variety of marks, each of which reflects a different muscular tension and type of arm motion. Gradually, over time and with practice, children gain more control over their motions and resulting marks. They learn to combine marks to make textures as well as to form basic shapes. They figure out that they can combine lines, textures, shapes and areas of color to break up and design the picture space.

Children from three different age groups paint people. A first-person painting, Denise Courtney, age 3½.

Self-portrait, Ellery Brown, grade 2.

Me and My Pet, Leah Hirsch, grade 5.

Students drew six different large shapes on their papers and then made each shape into a different person. Six characters, Nicole Henderson, grade 6, Buckland Shelburne Regional School, Massachusetts. Art teacher: Polly Anderson.

At about the time this development takes place (ages 3 to 6), children discover that their shape and line combinations suggest objects and movements in their world. They begin to draw people, animals, suns, vehicles, houses, plants and trees as well as movements such as explosions, wheels turning, a ball sailing through the air and rain. As children examine and experience their world and the objects and creatures within it, they elaborate on their ways of portraying objects, and their paintings become more detailed and more correctly proportioned. Of course, this only happens in painting if children are given many chances to use paint and to look at and evaluate the results.

As children grow older, they become much more critical of their work, and they need more input and information. The guidance and encouragement of an understanding teacher can make a tremendous difference in children's attitudes, interest and development in painting.

The chapters in this book are organized according to the ways children generally develop in paint-ing. The chapters in Part One are designed to encourage interaction with and exploration of the art elements — line, texture, shape, color, value and composition — which form the basis of all painting. The chapters in Part Two — Flowers and Still Life; The Environment; Animals; and People — suggest basic strategies for helping children to use paint to explore familiar objects and places in their world. The chapters in Part Three — Black Ink Painting of East Asia and Watercolors — introduce alternative painting materials, approaches and aesthetics. Part Four focuses on organizing painting materials and setting up to paint, as well as on looking at, thinking about and discussing artwork and the painting process.

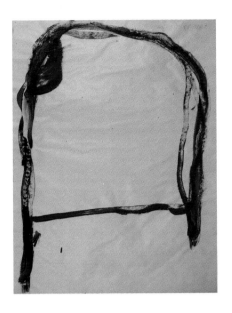

This series of easel paintings was painted by 3-year-old Emily Freeman-Daniels over the course of a week. These images show how one child explored ways of using painted lines to divide the paper space. They also show that something important happens when children paint at the easel.

Collecting children's paintings in a folder and taking them out every now and then is a good way to get a perspective on children's approaches to exploring paint. *A Papa Shoe and a Momma Shoe*, Emily Freeman-Daniels, age 3½.

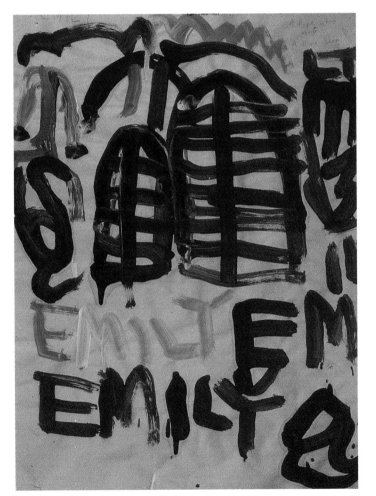

It is best to introduce a single art element or subject and explore it in depth, over time, before introducing the next one. For this reason, activities are arranged sequentially. Whenever possible, it is extremely rewarding to coordinate painting activities with major study units taking place in the classroom. Paintings about the weather will be much more meaningful, and the thinking process behind them more complex, when children are working on a scientific study of weather. Paintings of live models from the classroom make more sense when the class is studying the various kinds of joints in the human body and how they allow for particular movements and positions. Children can produce paintings of flowers, trees or insects that are very complex when they are based on knowledge.

When any child is having difficulty painting or

getting started, refer to the warm-up exercises in Part One and at the beginning of each of the other chapters. These warm-ups introduce basic concepts and techniques and open up possibilities for other projects. Taking a few minutes to warm up arm muscles and become familiar with paint consistency and setup is extremely helpful to painters of any age or skill level. The same holds true for musicians, dancers, and athletes. None of these performers would think of giving a concert or ballet or playing a match without stretching out and warming up first. Spending a few minutes on warm-up painting activities enables children to loosen up and become aware of the many different ways artists approach painting. Warm-up paintings are not meant to be saved, but, of course, they can be. Often, they provide a beginning structure or direction for more in-depth paintings.

Painting is an exercise in coming to terms with change. Painting is about making new discoveries.

The experience can be a glorious one or a frustrating one. It is important to prepare children to expect the unexpected. Encourage them to share their discoveries and learn from and use their "mistakes." Ask them, What happened while painting that you did not expect? How did you use that unexpected drip, blob, line or color? Encourage children to think of their "mistakes" as the paintings' way of telling them to try something else — make a drip into a free-form shape, add a texture or line, mix a new color, use the paintbrush in a different direction. Often, the best paintings develop from unintentional marks or colors that force the artist into a new way of working. Dialogue between a teacher and student or among students is important in helping children become aware of their accomplishments. Dialogue also helps children feel confident about their ability to paint. For this reason, suggested strategies for giving positive feedback and additional input are part of each chapter.

This 20-month-old is enjoying the experience of watching her arm and body motions become visible marks on paper. Warm-up exercises at the beginning of each chapter in Part One can help both children and adults connect with the joy and wonder of these early free-painting attempts.

Part One
Approaches to Painting

The art elements—line, texture, shape, color and value—are part of every painting. They are the building blocks from which paintings are made. The same elements are the keys to unlocking and understanding the vision of an artist and the way a particular painting affects the viewer. Composition refers to how art elements are arranged in any given work of art.

It is by focusing on one element at a time and developing skill in using and looking for that element in the environment and in works of art that children can grow and develop as painters, as communicators and as people who understand and appreciate the achievements of other artists.

Me in My Snow Clothes,
Courtney Watson, grade 1.

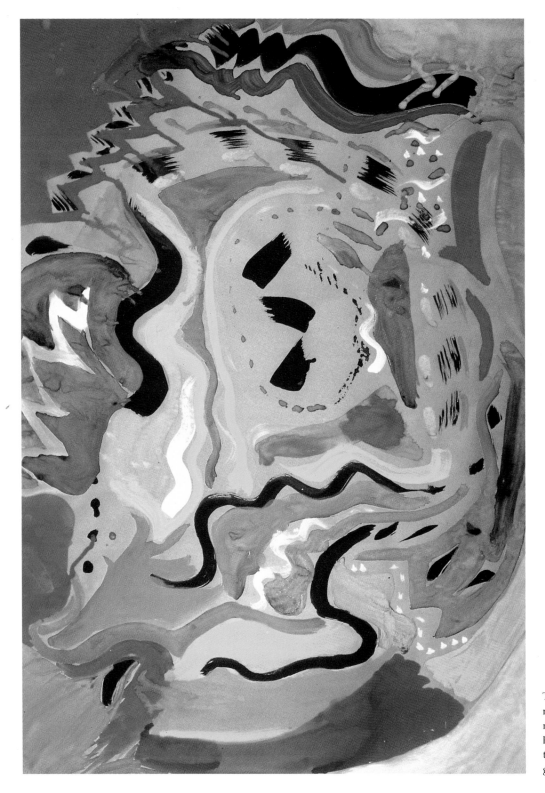

This painting serves as a
reminder that there are
many different kinds of
lines and brushstrokes to
try. Alethia Donohue,
grade 5.

8

1 Exploring the Brushstroke

Every painting originates with a single brushstroke or mark. One way of thinking about a painting is to look at it as simply the sum of its brushstrokes. Feeling confident about holding and using the brush is one key to enjoying, understanding, and beginning the painting process.

Introducing painting by focusing on the brushstroke eliminates the need for using many different colors. In fact, having more than one color to begin with is distracting. Painting with only one color encourages children to experiment with the different kinds of marks they can create with a brush and to think about how and where they hold the brush. In initial painting activities, using only one color allows the teacher to introduce paint preparation, distribution and cleanup procedures in the simplest manner possible.

The brush is an extension of the arm and hand. The brushstroke is a result of the motions the arm and hand make. The length and nature of the stroke depends in part on which joint of the arm is used, the size and type of brush, and on how freely or tightly the brush is held. Students become aware of these subtleties when teachers call attention to them. Focus on one aspect of using the brush at a time, calling attention to others after brushwork has begun and children are ready for more input.

With a brush and a dark color of paint, demonstrate a long, straight brushstroke using only your shoulder joint. Place your free hand on the shoulder joint of the arm holding the brush. That way, you can feel the arm motion in two ways. Talk about the kind of stroke you are making, and emphasize the length. Ask the children to pretend they are holding brushes, and have them try the exercises in the air along with you. Move your free hand down to your elbow, and demonstrate the same stroke using only the elbow as the impetus for the stroke. Be sure not to let your wrist move! Try the same stroke with your wrist and then your fingers. Use your opposite hand to keep the other joints from moving.

Be sure to demonstrate, and allow the class as a whole to try, dramatically different strokes such as broken, zigzag and curvy. Children will quickly see and feel what a difference using a particular joint makes in the size and quality of their brushstrokes. By helping children connect their arm motions with the resulting marks, the whole painting process becomes much more concrete. The following exercises emphasize different aspects of using a brush. It is preferable to stand up while trying these beginning exercises, as standing allows the arm to move more freely. However, the exercises will also work if students are seated.

Getting in Touch with Your Painting Arm

MATERIALS: One ⅜" easel brush for each student, containers of paint and several sheets of newsprint for each child. It is great for students to work on 18" x 24" paper, but 12" x 18" is fine too. This warm-up exercise can also be done directly on newspaper and thrown away. After some practice, hand each student a sheet of white paper to try a final painting, then fill it in with primary colors, or select places to paint with one color.

It is helpful to follow the warm-up exercise by asking children to tell you which joints they usually use for painting, which joint they would use to paint big shapes and which joint they would use to paint tiny details.

The way students hold their brushes also makes a difference. You might demonstrate a firm grip and a loose grip while discussing the probable result of each. As children work, encourage them to experiment with all the options. In particular, help students with very tight grips loosen up by gently moving their painting arms in the air until they relax a little. Help students with very little control to try tightening their grips and sliding their hands closer to the front of the brushes. Ask, "When would you want to use a looser, freer grip? When might you want to move your hand down towards the bristles so that you have more control?"

Usually, painters hold their brushes in the middle or thickest part of the handle. Most of the exercises in this book use ⅜" easel brushes. A ½" brush would also work well.

For more control, try gripping the brush farther down on the handle.

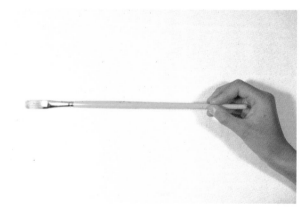

When working more freely, artists sometimes use a looser grip, holding their brushes at the ends of the handles.

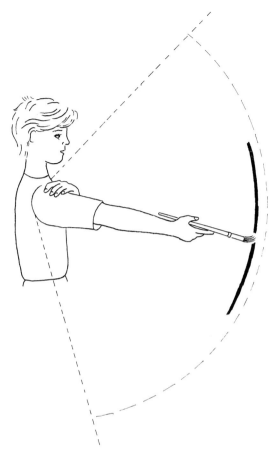

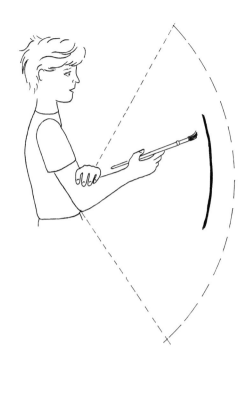

Paint a few lines using only your shoulder joint. Be sure you are using the correct joint by holding onto it with your free hand.

Paint a few lines using only your elbow joint. Remember to hold your elbow with your free hand.

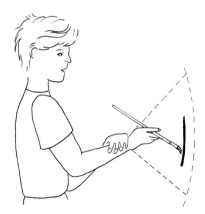

Try painting from only your wrist joint.

Try painting using only your finger joints.

Developing a Brushstroke Vocabulary

Assigning descriptive words or names to basic strokes gives students and teachers a common vocabulary for talking about art. Straight, curvy, zigzag, dotted, broken, branching, crisscrossed, fast, slow, spiral, dabbed, dotted, graduated, thick, thin, squiggly, strong, weak, horizontal, vertical and diagonal are all words that can be used to describe marks. Children especially enjoy inventing names to describe particular marks. "Radiator" lines, "cage" lines and "curly" lines are a few examples of names children have assigned to different line configurations. During the demonstration part of the following activity, either paint a line and ask children to name it or ask a student to come to the front of the room to demonstrate a particular line, such as a "branching" or "thick-to-thin" line.

Once a name and image are connected in a student's mind, refer to that common vocabulary. As you circulate through the room, you might say, "I see you tried out the zigzag line and the dotted line. You made big ones, little ones and medium-size ones; you made them up and down and sideways. Which line will you try next — a squiggly or branching line? Oh, you'd rather try a curved line? That's a good idea."

Check to see whether you have different sizes of each stroke. Try the same strokes, but make them go in different directions. Try the same exercise with a different kind of stroke.

When brushstroke experiments are complete, children may select the ones they like best to fill in with color. *Crazy Colored,* Sarah Rundquist, grade 4.

Make at least eight different kinds of brushstrokes or lines. Keep each line separate. Display a chart of brushstrokes as a visual reminder of different kinds of lines to try.

Repeat each line and change its size. Connect all lines. At this point, children might enjoy the challenge of working with a very thin brush.

Relating Lines to Weather Conditions

Lines can be used to show a variety of weather conditions. Encourage children to think about ways an artist might interpret rain, wind, thunder and lightning with lines. Have children demonstrate a particular weather condition using arm movements to show the pathway of leaves swirling in a strong gust of wind, fog settling over the mountains, rays of sunlight shining through the clouds after a downpour, whitecaps on a stormy sea and snow falling silently on a winter's night. Look at a variety of paintings and photographs that show different weather conditions. Ask children to tell you what the weather is in two or three paintings and to point out what clues in the paintings they used to arrive at their conclusions.

Using a chart is a quick way to help children focus on one specific weather condition at a time. It opens up many possibilities for thinking about, and painting, a variety of weather conditions and different kinds of movements in simple ways.

Painting a Weather Chart

MATERIALS: Jars of black paint, a medium brush for each student (size 7 round works well), 18″ x 24″ pieces of newsprint folded into sixteen rectangles. (Younger children may divide their papers into eight spaces instead of sixteen.)

How does this artist let you know that it is a rainy day? Notice the clouds, the rain, the droopy bare trees and sagging roofs, the puddles and reflections in the puddles. What time of year is it in this painting? Charles Burchfield, *Factory Town, Trees.* Gouache on paper 23¼″ x 19½″ (59 cm x 49.5 cm). Courtesy of Colby College Museum of Art, anonymous gift.

Think about the weather conditions in each box.

6-sided snowflake	gentle snow	blizzard	hail
icicles	gentle breeze	strong wind	tornado
clouds	falling leaves	fog	thunder and lightning
close-up of raindrops	rainstorm	sun from behind a cloud	very hot sun

Then paint lines in each box on your paper that show your impression of the weather condition. Students should compare their interpretations with those of their classmates.

After children have completed a weather chart, they are ready to combine a few of their linear impressions into a painting about a particular kind of weather condition. These paintings are usually completed fairly quickly. *A Tornado*, Brita Dempsey, grade 5.

This chalk painting of a storm was drawn on very wet paper. Children first used sponges to make their papers shiny and wet. Claire Zar-Kessler, age 5.

This 8-year-old special needs child used black, white and blue paint to mix dark and light values in his stormy weather painting. Art teacher: Amelia Hayes.

Relating Lines to Sounds

Music is a terrific stimulus for exploring various aspects of painting, especially for exploring different brushstrokes. Each group of instruments — woodwinds, strings, brass and percussion — produce sounds that differ in character, suggesting a variety of movements and lines to the painter. The beat in a piece of music is like a pulse, and can suggest a structure or framework to the visual artist. That framework might be varied by different rhythms, or ways of dividing the space between the beats, and by the tempo which speeds up and slows down like the heart. Sounds can be loud (forte) or soft (piano). A crescendo is a sound that grows louder and stronger, while a diminuendo is a sound that fades out. Sounds can be broken or connected. Staccato sounds are detached or broken and are often short, strong and fast. Sounds played in a legato fashion are connected and smooth.

You might choose one or two elements important to the composition of both music and art to stress at a time, adding another element or two as children progress. The melody, contrast between sounds, and repetition of sounds can all suggest

visual interpretations to children when they are guided in their listening.

Music teachers are usually accommodating when asked for suggestions of selections to play as stimuli for an art lesson. It is helpful to have pieces of music that are very different in feeling. *Rumanian Folk Dances for Orchestra* by Béla Bartók, contrasts well with piano selections by Claude Debussy or with *The Rite of Spring* by Igor Stravinsky. *Peter and the Wolf* by Sergey Prokofkiev, *The Nutcracker* by Pyotr Tchaikovsky and *The Young Person's Guide to the Orchestra* by Benjamin Britten are selections that include many different instruments with recurring themes. They also include a variety of fast and slow parts. Antonio Vivaldi's *The Four Seasons* includes rich contrasts within each section. Japanese classical music, Native American flute music and medieval instrumental music often present new and unusual sounds to children. Play a musical selection that you enjoy, and try moving your arm to it. Try sketching lines to it. You will be able to judge quickly whether or not it has enough variety for a painting exercise. Avoid music that is too rousing! In general it is handy to have a few musical selections available to play while children are working. Some of the many

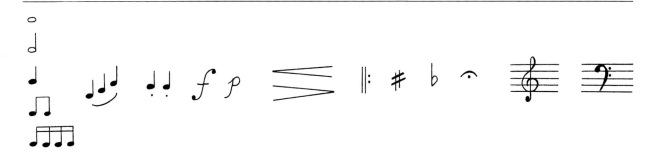

Musical notations are helpful to use when talking about music and art. They are also especially lovely line configurations. From top to bottom at left, the musical notations stand for whole, half, quarter, eighth and sixteenth notes. The curved line under several notes indicates legato. Dots indicate staccato. *F,* or *forte,* means loud. *P,* or *piano,* means soft. Hairpins indicate crescendo and diminuendo sounds. Two lines with two dots mean repeat. A sharp before the note raises it a half step. The flat lowers the note a half step. A fermata is a hold or pause. The G and F clefs fix the pitches. G clef, or treble clef, is where a child typically speaks or sings. F clef, or bass clef, is where a man usually speaks or sings. Children who read music might enjoy including musical notations in their paintings done to music.

Kandinsky, whose first artistic training was in music, often spoke of his paintings as if they were musical compositions. He believed that painting, like music, is a means of communication. He used the elements of art — line, point and color — as a symbolic visual language in the same way that music is a language of sounds. Though the lines in this drawing may look like casual scribbles, they were carefully drawn and arranged. As students listen to musical selections, ask them to think about lines or marks they can make to suggest a particular sound. Do they see any lines in this painting that might suggest fast, broken, staccato sounds or smooth, long, legato sounds? Can they find any lines that look like they might be quiet sounds or very loud sounds? Do they see any lines that suggest repeating sounds? Wassily Kandinsky, *Untitled (Drawing for "Diagram 17")*, 1925. Black ink on ivory paper, Courtesy of the Mount Holyoke College Art Museum, South Hadley, Massachusetts.

tapes used for meditation are helpful in calming a class.

Ask children to demonstrate how they might paint a sound. How could you show a slow, dreamy melody? What kind of mark could you use to suggest the sound of a violin, the clash of cymbals or the beat of a drum? Be accepting of all honest answers, as each student responds to music in a personal way.

Play a piece of music and ask children to close their eyes and listen. Ask them to try moving their arms as if they were conducting the piece. Introduce contrasting arm movements such as high (to signal high-pitched sounds) and low (for low sounds), hard (forte) and soft (piano), curving and straight, broken (staccato) and flowing (legato). Ask children how they might show a crescendo or diminuendo using arm motions.

Refrain from handing out paintbrushes until students have spent a few moments listening and allowing the feeling of the selection to sink in. Suggest that students choose a few sounds from the many they are hearing and try to reflect those sounds in line. This may take practice, so an extra piece of paper for practicing each selection might be necessary.

Painting to Music

MATERIALS: A paintbrush for each student, several 18" x 24" sheets of newsprint, manila, or white paper for every student and one color of paint to start with. A few other colors, such as the primaries and white, may be used later to paint between the lines.

Instruct students to close their eyes and listen to the music: Listen for the melody or main theme of the music. Listen for contrasting sounds — forte/piano, high-pitched/low-pitched, staccato/legato, crescendo/diminuendo. Listen for repeating sounds or rhythms. Move your arm as if you were the conductor and as if you were leading each instrument, telling it when to come in and how it should sound. Be selective. Listen for one or two kinds of sounds at a time. Once you begin painting, remember to use the whole paper. Touch the edges.

This fourth-grader uses a large brush to paint to music. She works here on a very large piece of brown mural paper.

Children were asked to fill in the shapes created by the lines and to relate the colors they selected to the mood of the music. *Garden of Colors*, Leah Hirsch, grade 4.

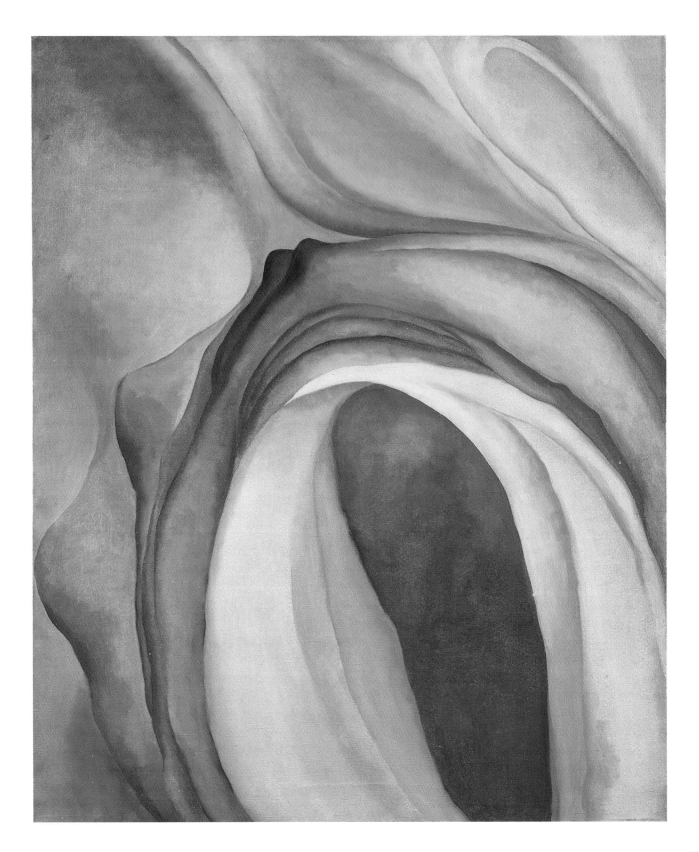

As an alternative to black paint on white paper, try using white paint on a piece of colored construction paper while painting to music. After paintings dry, use oil pastels to add color and convey the mood of the music. Painting in the colors with oil pastels enables students to achieve beautiful effects with blending. When using oil pastels over the white lines, children can create delicate tints. If you try this, remember to pad the working surface with a thick section of newspaper. *The Dance of the Sugarplum Fairies,* (from *The Nutcracker* by Tchaikosvky) Emily Scaife, grade 5.

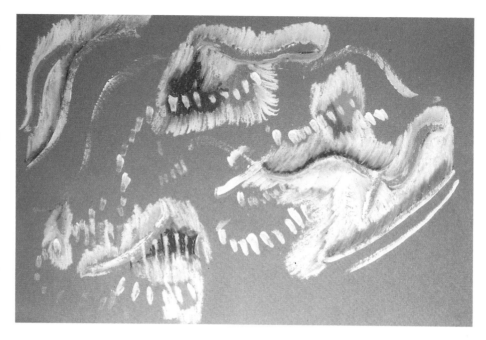

Summary

Color seems to be the art element that relates to music in this painting. In 1929, Georgia O'Keeffe said, "I found that I could say things with color and shapes that I couldn't say in any other way — things that I had no words for." Encourage children to think about what feelings they wish to convey in their paintings and to select colors that convey those emotions to them. Georgia O'Keeffe, *Music Pink and Blue II,* 1919. Oil on canvas, 35½" x 29" (90 cm x 74 cm). Collection Emily Fisher Landau, New York. Courtesy of the Georgia O'Keeffe Foundation. Photo courtesy of Malcolm Varon, NYC, ca. 1987.

Paying attention to where the brush is held and to which joints of the body propel the brushstroke helps students connect their own motions with the resulting painted marks. By trying new holding positions and new ways of moving, children can expand their brushstroke options and learn ways of controlling the brush.

Helping children develop and use descriptive words enables them to evaluate and communicate about their discoveries and to add to a growing art vocabulary. Straight, curved, zigzag, dotted, broken, branching, crisscrossed, spiral, dabbed, squiggly, graduated, thick, thin, long, short, light, dark, delicate, bold, strong, weak, horizontal, vertical and diagonal are all words that can be used to describe different kinds of marks or brushstrokes.

Using a verbal and visual line vocabulary is a way not only to explore weather and sound, but also to make the art element *line* more concrete. Relating abstract lines to sounds and forces in a child's world helps children become more sensitive to their environment.

In this black and white photograph of Bonnard's colorful painting (see p. 28), it is easy to see the varied brushstrokes. There are many sizes of dots, dabs and lines. Groupings of brushstrokes go in different directions enabling us to differentiate one area from another. Pierre Bonnard, *Landscape in Normandy*, 1920 (completed later). Oil on canvas, 24⅝" x 32" (63 cm x 81 cm). Smith College Museum of Art, Northampton, Massachusetts.

2 Emphasizing Texture

Every surface has a texture. The term *texture* is used to describe the quality of a surface — how a surface would feel if you touched it. A painted surface might be smooth, rough, prickly or bumpy. Texture can also refer to the way paint has been applied to a surface. Sometimes painters use palette knives to apply thick globs of paint. Sometimes paint is spattered onto a surface. Sometimes the brush is used to add lines, dabs and areas of paint. In some instances, painters mix other substances, such as sand, into their paintings, or paint over collaged surfaces to create texture.

Texture not only activates the sense of touch, but also the sense of vision. It can refer to the way something looks as if it would feel. In other words, a painting of a rocky shore can appear to be extremely jagged and full of sharp edges, when, in fact, the surface of the painting is smooth. A woman's dress might appear to be made of the softest velvet, but the surface of the painting still just feels like canvas.

A texture is made up of many similar elements placed closely together. Fur on a kitten, grass on a hillside, pine needles on the ground, and a head of curly hair are all textured surfaces made up of linear elements. A pile of shells, pebbles on a beach and autumn leaves on the ground are all textured areas that can be suggested by painted dots or shapes.

Looking at the World with Texture Eyes

By focusing on texture as a way to approach painting, you cause children to look at their environment in a very specific way. You ask them to look at the world with "texture eyes," or from a texture viewpoint only. Once children have developed a visual and verbal texture vocabulary and an understanding of the concept of texture, you can call on their experience and integrate texture into other activities. Then, texture can be one of many elements children are asked to think about when painting. But if you really want children to develop a rich understanding of the varied ways to use texture in painting, you must first focus only on texture.

An easy and effective way to approach texture is to have youngsters make a texture chart. Start by generating a list of textures and writing the examples on the board. Sand, cornfields, grain and other plantings, ocean waves, fire, a spider's web, wood grain, bark and trees in the distance are all textures that occur in the landscape. Many rich textures and patterns exist in the animal kingdom. Dots on a leopard, cheetah or dalmatian; stripes on a tiger, raccoon or zebra; scales on a fish; odd shapes on a giraffe; and, markings on a turtle's shell are only a few. The difference between pattern and texture can be confusing. Often the two overlap, as they do on many animals, and in fabrics and building materials. Knitted material, corduroy, tweed and herringbone fabrics, plaids, braided rugs, carpet and wicker are all man-made textures. Building materials such as bricks, shingles, stucco, clapboards, metal and wooden fences and trellises, pavement and stone all have distinctive textures. Making a chart gives children an opportunity to concentrate on one texture at a time.

Painting a Texture Chart

MATERIALS: Jars of paint, easel brushes, 18″ x 24″ sheets of newsprint or white paper folded into sixteen rectangles.

After a little experience at creating textured areas with a brush, children are ready to use their textures in a painting assignment. Instructing students to paint only textures, not outlines, is the most important direction for this activity.

A painted texture is actually one mark or brushstroke repeated many times. In order to paint a texture, it is first helpful to identify one kind of stroke and repeat it.

Point out or demonstrate that textures can be created using different parts of the bristle. This texture was created using the tip of an easel brush.

A texture made by pressing the entire bristle firmly onto the paper.

A texture made by using the skinny edge of an easel brush.

Making a collection of textured objects from both the natural and man-made environments is a good way to develop an awareness of texture.

Fold a large sheet of newsprint in half four times. When opened, you should have sixteen rectangles. Here is an example of a completed texture chart. Working from actual objects makes a big difference in the variety of textures a person is able to perceive and create. Students should paint the line and shape textures they see, not outlines of the objects.

A painting is more effective when textures are carried all the way to the edges of the paper. Sarah Rundquist, grade 4.

Calling attention to the kinds of building materials used in different parts of a house helps give children ideas about specific kinds of textures. Alex Batten, grade 5.

Landscapes and Waterscapes

MATERIALS: Jars of black paint, brushes, 18" x 24" white paper.

Limiting variables, such as the number of colors available for use, helps children concentrate on one concept at a time. When working simply — with black paint on a light surface, or in the reverse, with white paint on black paper — even young children seem able to understand the idea of using their brushes to suggest textures and movements. In fact, children will be much more attuned to subtle textures after completing a texture painting. It is fun to try one painting using black paint on white paper and a second using white paint on black paper. Giving children a chance to repeat an activity with a slight variation enables them to become good at a particular task and to learn by practice. That is certainly how most artists perfect their craft; children rarely get the same opportunity.

To achieve contrast in your painting, make some textures open with lots of space between the brushstrokes and some textures more concentrated and darker by placing brushstrokes close together. Think about painting the object the way it grows, moves or is built.

One way to paint birds is to pay attention to their interesting textures and patterns. Peacock, Beth Verson, grade 4.

After completing a texture painting using black paint on white paper, children were asked to reverse the colors and use white tempera paint on black paper. Making the same textures big in the foreground and smaller in the background creates an illusion of distance. *Night Scene,* Sara Schiefflin, grade 4.

Children are often skeptical about using a texture approach to painting animals. But they are often equally surprised by how well they can do using this approach. Lizard, Alethia Donohue, grade 5.

Even with all the practice, once children are presented with an array of colors, their sensitivity to texture seems to get lost among color choices. After many attempts to find a way to help children use their texture sensitivity when working in color, the following activity — based on paintings by the Impressionists — has been found to be successful. The process and resulting paintings have been exciting and dramatic.

Children enjoy the immediacy, vibrancy and bright colors of paintings by the Impressionists. However, it was not only the colors the Impressionists used that began a new way of painting; it was also their brushstrokes. In their quest to capture impressions of reality as opposed to photographic images, many painters of this period used brushstrokes to convey a sense of movement and liveliness.

Encourage children to think about the strokes they are making as they add the element of color to their texture paintings. It is helpful to have many paintings by the Impressionists available for study. The brushstrokes in Vincent van Gogh's paintings are especially evident and varied. Call children's attention to the brush textures that different artists used to show water, sunlight, grass, foliage, flowers and wind. Point out the direction of the brushstrokes in each case.

Adding Color to Texture Paintings

MATERIALS: White texture paintings on black paper from the previous activity, medium brushes, a variety of other colors of paint.

As you add a color over a textured area, be sure to paint in the same direction as the white brushstrokes. Paint using the same kind of stroke used in that area of the painting. Paint each color in more than one place to unify the painting. Fill the page with color.

Notice that the colors of this painting are predominantly different greens — yellow-greens, blue-greens and grass-greens. Where is the sun in this painting? Pierre Bonnard, *Landscape in Normandy*, 1920 (completed later). Oil on canvas, 24⅝" x 32" (63 cm x 81 cm). Courtesy of the Smith College Museum of Art, Northampton, Massachusetts.

When painting over white brushstrokes, a little of the white paint mixes with the color, creating a sparkling effect against the black paper. Claire Topal, grade 5.

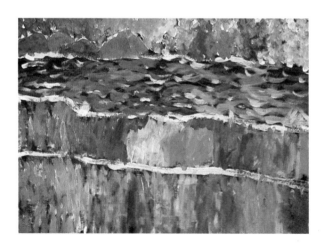

Using the brush to paint in different directions helps make one area stand out. *Reflections*, Nick Burk, grade 6.

Summary

Providing time for children to observe and make a few different textures is crucial to helping them understand how to use texture in their paintings. By concentrating only on texture, children will soon see that the size of their marks, the direction of those marks and the spacing between marks makes a big difference in the kind of textures they can make. Using concepts of size, direction and spacing also helps children make one textured area stand out from another.

With practice, children will discover that where they hold the brush, which part of the bristle they use and how hard they press also affects the kinds of textures that they can make. With guidance, children will learn to look more closely, to approach painting in a new way and to be more attuned to texture in their environment and their painting.

The hard-edged geometric shapes in this painting are parts of man-made objects. Look for the curvy and straight edges of shapes that make up parts of the table, guitar and bottle. Ask students to pick out shapes that repeat several times. Look for L's, D's, S's, triangles and rectangles; notice the ways the artist has varied their size and placement. It is also interesting to notice the way the artist has interchanged positive and negative shapes. Pablo Picasso, *Table, Guitar, and Bottle (La Table)*, 1919. Oil on canvas, 50" x 29½" (127 cm x 75 cm). Smith College Museum of Art, Northampton, Massachusetts.

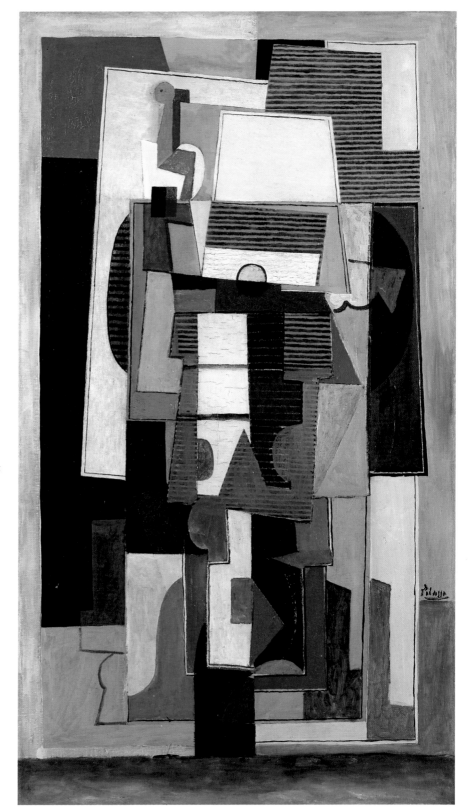

3 Focusing on Shape

To paint is to create shapes. When a brush filled with paint meets a surface and moves around, a shape is formed. Once paint is applied to paper or canvas, those painted areas stand out as positive shapes. What is left over in the background is a negative shape. Mature painters are conscious not only of the painted shapes they are applying to a surface, but also of the negative shapes being formed at the same time. Most children are oblivious to this connection unless it is called to their attention. Once children's awareness of negative shapes has been heightened, they enjoy looking for negative shapes and begin to see them in their environment.

Every object has a shape. Regular, or geometric, shapes include circles, squares, rectangles and triangles. Many man-made objects such as windows, doorknobs, dishes and furniture are made up of geometric shapes. All other shapes are categorized as irregular, or freeform. Freeform shapes found in nature are referred to as "organic" because they are created by the growth of living organisms. Organic shapes can be quite complex, and no two of them

Soft-edged freeform shapes suggest organic shapes found in the natural world. The artist was seeking to express the universal rhythms of a variety of life forces. He was sensitive to the motions of wind, water and other elements of the landscape and used color and form as abstract ways of communicating what he felt. Arthur G. Dove, *Happy Landscape*, 1937. Oil on canvas, 10" x 13⁵⁄₁₆" (25 cm × 35.5 cm). Smith College Museum of Art, Northampton, Massachusetts.

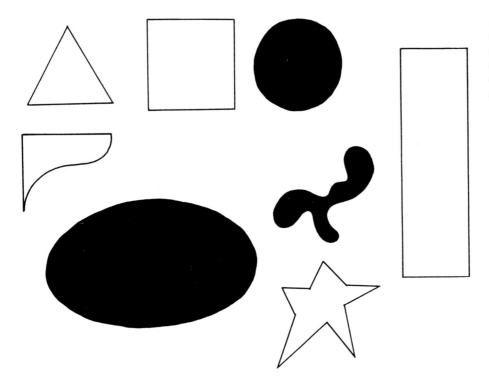

are exactly alike. The shapes of continents, countries and rivers on a map; clouds; leaves; rocks; bones and body parts such as hands and feet are referred to as organic shapes when seen from an abstract point of view.

Painting and shapes go hand in hand. Artists often explore shapes in and of themselves as subject matter for painting. Perhaps that is because there are so many kinds of shapes and ways to vary them. Shapes can have curvy edges, straight edges or both. Shapes can be enormous or tiny, dark or light, soft-edged or hard-edged. The edges of shapes can also be blurred or so indistinct that you cannot tell where one shape or area ends and the next begins. Shapes can be opaque or translucent. Shapes can touch, overlap or stand alone.

In the preceding chapters, focusing on linear aspects of painting gave students a chance to explore what they could do with a brush and with ways of moving the arm and hand to produce differ-ent kinds of strokes. Focusing on texture gave students cause to repeat those strokes and arm motions again and again in order to change the quality of the painted surface.

Focusing on shape offers students an opportunity to concentrate on what happens after the brush has touched the painting's surface. Focusing on shape involves moving paint around on the picture plane and on breaking that plane down into areas of color. It gives students a forum for exploring how shapes come into being — as outlines that get filled in or as blobs that work themselves into pleasing masses of color.

Demonstrating Ways to Paint Shapes

Be sure to demonstrate the outline and blob methods of painting shapes. Make sure children try out both approaches. Demonstrate what happens when one painted shape touches another. Share your delight in making a new color by blending the edges of the two shapes. Point out negative shapes that have been created by your positive shapes, and fill some in. Deliberately make a mistake, and use that mistake in a new way.

Demonstrating is an effective way to spark interest and convey information. Demonstrations should be basic and fairly simple. They should show only what children need to know in order to begin. Demonstrations should also be open-ended. They should suggest several approaches to solving a particular problem. An effective demonstration is also dependent on your enthusiasm and ability to relate an activity to the children's experience. At the same time, you do not want to show too much or be intimidating. If comments such as "You're so good" begin to surface, it is definitely time to stop. You want children to say, "That looks exciting. It also looks easy. I understand the directions. I know what I want to do. Let me begin!"

The following activity is designed to help children find a quick entrance into a painting and, once there, to encourage them to experiment with the wonderful feeling of paint as it moves around on paper. It is also intended to help children pay attention to the negative shapes they are simultaneously creating in the background. Another goal is to help children become aware that there is more than one way of working and to begin to identify which way of creating shapes they prefer. Experimenting with two techniques for painting shapes helps children gain awareness of how they like to paint.

This child at the La Villetta School in Reggio Emilia, Italy, uses the outline method in his painting, which appears to be based on the rectangle and square. This is a painting of the field from a bird's-eye view.

Help children find a starting place by asking them to tell you which kind of shape they will paint first. Be aware that plans may change as children begin to work. Some children find it difficult to paint precise shapes. Encourage them to watch what is happening in their paintings and go with the flow of the paint. Accept and enjoy the interesting and different ways children interpret this lesson.

Shapes Come to Life

MATERIALS: Paint in the three primary colors — red, yellow and blue, medium-size brushes, water dishes, 11" x 17" white paper. *Note: If you trim an inch off the length and width of standard-sized paper before students begin painting, it will be easier and faster to mount the finished paintings.*

Paint a large shape using the outline method, and fill it in. Touch an edge or a corner of the paper so that you can clearly see the negative shape of the rest of the paper.

Paint a shape using the blob method. Move the paint around and out in different directions until you have a shape that pleases you.

Paint at least two shapes with each color. Add interest to the painting by varying shapes. Paint big and tiny shapes. Paint curvy and straight-edged shapes. Paint geometric and freeform shapes. Find some negative shapes in the background and paint them in.

When one colored area touches another, try blending the edges to create a new color and shape.

Fill your paper with colorful shapes. Paint around some shapes and inside others. Overlap shapes.

When the first few children have covered their papers, it is a good idea to stop the entire class for a moment and take stock of what has happened. Hold up a few paintings that are quite different in nature, and comment on ways that children have varied shapes. Celebrate the differences you see. Reinforce art concepts by pointing out, or asking children to point out, where they have tried negative shapes, dramatic size differences, overlapping, outlining and contrasting light and dark shapes.

You can build children's confidence by delighting in the discoveries they make. You can make a process experience richer by giving children a chance to use their art terms as they share their observations with other members of the class. Encourage children to describe how they created particular shapes. Ask children to discuss difficulties they had in controlling the paint. Ask children which methods of creating masses of color worked best for creating precise, hard-edged shapes and which worked best when blurry-edged shapes were desired.

As children complete these paintings, encourage them to stand back and look at their work. Looking for a center of interest is a dramatic way to begin. "Close your eyes. Open your eyes. What part of your painting did you see first?" Ask children to try this several times noting how their attention moves from the center of interest to other areas within the paintings. Demonstrate the way this kind of looking enables the viewer to move deeper and deeper into a painting. Ask children to think about why their eye moves in a particular pathway. Is it a repeating color, shape or line that attracts their attention? Allow time for children to try looking for the center of interest in their own paintings and in their neighbors' paintings.

Shape paintings can be considered finished works, or they can be taken one step farther. You might point out that one reason so many artists enjoy exploring shapes is that shapes are evocative. Because all objects have shape, it follows that certain shapes remind us of objects. Freeform shapes suggest natural forms such as people, animals, plants and landscapes. Geometric shapes suggest buildings, machines and other man-made objects. As a follow-up to a shape painting activity, children can be encouraged to brainstorm about their own painted shapes and to bring their ideas to life by adding details and shapes to their paintings with a small easel or watercolor brush and black paint.

Emphasize the use of small brushes and the idea of overpainting. This gives children the opportunity to find out what small brushes can do that big brushes cannot. It also gives children a chance to take a second look at their previous work.

Overpainting with Small Brushes

MATERIALS: Black paint and small easel or watercolor brushes. White paint and small brushes can also be made available to give students more options.

Direct students to turn their paintings around, and look at them from different directions. They should look for movements and forms that catch their interest and suggest objects in the world. Using small brushes and black and white paint, students should bring their shapes to life. Instruct students to: Overpaint small shapes on top of large ones. Outline a shape. Connect shapes with lines. Add line and shape textures. Create either a nonobjective or realistic picture. Finally, have students think up titles for their paintings.

Looking at the World with Shape Eyes

Looking at, and painting in, important shapes is often the first step in developing any composition — especially compositions of still-life objects, animals or buildings. Once artists have roughed in their major shapes, they refine those shapes and add other smaller shapes as well as other colors, lines and textures to further define their subjects.

Before artists can do this, they must analyze the scenes or objects for their component shapes. A special way of looking is required to break down scenes or objects in this manner. It is a way of looking that artists are especially good at, but that most people do not do naturally. Most people must be shown how to look and asked to develop that visual skill or way of looking.

Being visually literate includes looking through eyes that find rectangles, squares, triangles and trap-ezoids instead of specific things like doors, windows and roofs on a house, or through eyes that can isolate freeform, curvy-edged shapes instead of legs and arms. As a teacher of visual arts, you need to help people learn the skill of seeing in this special way.

Children seem to understand intuitively when a teacher asks them to put on their "shape eyes" as they look at whatever subject they are about to paint. "What shapes can you find? Which is the largest shape? Which is the smallest? Which shapes repeat? How many rectangles can you find? Can you find any half circles, pointy shapes, curved shapes?" These are all questions that help children develop looking skills. Build in time to listen to what children are saying as they respond to these kinds of questions. Their responses tell you what the next direction, question or clarification might be.

The freely painted shapes and lines in this brush drawing are lively and expressive. Drawing with the brush is a quick way to create a large plan for painting in at a later time. Raoul Dufy, *The Duomo, Florence*, ca. 1922. Watercolor over graphite, 19⅝" x 25⁷⁄₁₆" (50 cm x 65 cm). Smith College Museum of Art, Northampton, Massachusetts.

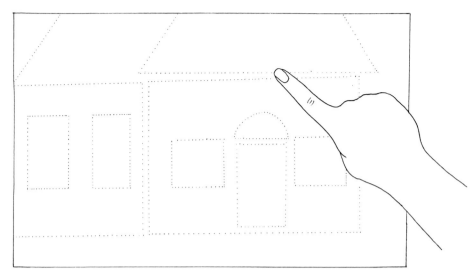

Encourage children to use a finger or dry paintbrush to "sketch" the main shapes in their compositions before making any marks on paper. This simple and quick exercise saves much time and enables children to quickly get a feel for size relationships. Thinking through a painting is a skill that can be applied to many painting activities.

Using the subject of houses as a springboard is an excellent way to begin painting realistic subject matter with young children. Houses are easy to analyze in terms of shapes. A few pictures of houses or public buildings that show a variety of shapes spark the visualization process. A chart with some basic house shapes is helpful too. The theme of houses can be expanded to include fantasy or dream houses, palaces, castles, haunted houses or pictures of the children's homes.

It is always preferable to show more than one approach to solving a problem. According to a school psychologist, this is quite important because different children perceive the same subject in markedly different ways. One way to begin a house painting is to fit the largest main shapes onto the page, then work down to the smaller shapes. With this approach, a student can easily fit a whole house onto the paper. This approach emphasizes thinking in terms of the main large shapes. It seems to work better when painting from memory.

Another way to paint a house is to begin with a small detail, such as the shape of the door, and work out from there adding other details such as windows, molding, a doorknob, doorbell, mailbox, portico, steps, shutters, etc. The goal would be to include as many details as possible. Fitting the whole house on the paper probably would not occur with this approach. This approach works especially well when painting houses from direct observation. Demonstrate both approaches, then let children decide which they will use. Or, try two brush drawings, one using each approach, and choose one drawing to paint with other colors.

Painting Houses

MATERIALS: 16" x 22" sheets of manila paper, easel brushes, water dishes, a variety of colors of paint — be sure to include many tints, some shades, white, gray, black and light blue. There should be a wide range of colors at each painting station.

Starting with the Main Large Shape

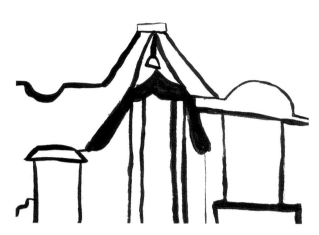

Choose one color of paint to brush-draw the basic shapes. Draw the largest outside shapes first — the frame of the house and the roof or roofs.

Add the smaller shapes of windows, doors, porches, shutters, chimneys, etc. Add any railings, porches, stairways, gates, columns, TV antennae, etc.

Fill the shapes in your painting with imaginative colors. Paint the sky, ground, bushes, trees, lampposts and mailboxes, too. Paint the entire page; no paper should show. Ariana Wohl, grade 5.

Younger children's paintings are often free and expressive. Robbie Gilman, kindergarten, Jackson Street School, Northampton, Massachusetts. Art teacher: Jacklyn Coe.

For some children, house shape paintings can easily turn into vibrant and free paintings — which is what often happens when abstract artists paint from realistic subject matter. Alison Batten, grade 1.

Starting with a Detail

Children studied windows and doors on Colonial houses in Old Deerfield Village. Each child then drew an ornate window or door, cut the window or door so that it would open and drew an inside scene on a separate piece of paper, which was later pasted to the back of the window. Watercolor paints were used to add color. *Open Window with Inside Scene,* Teresa Cavanna, grade 3, Buckland Shelburne Regional School. Art teacher: Polly Anderson.

Children in the upper grades are usually more detailed in their paintings of buildings. They are also more thoughtful about placing and mixing colors for special effects. Claire Topal, grade 6.

Summary

By trying out several different approaches to making shapes, children can begin to identify a few specifics about the style in which they enjoy painting. Shape exercises also help children to look at works of art by a variety of painters with an eye to picking out styles of painting and discussing a variety of approaches. Students should have an opportunity to try both the blob and outline approaches to painting a shape. They may also be encouraged to experiment with other ways of making a shape such as swirling the brush, stroking or dabbing. Classifying shapes into hard-edged versus soft-edged, geometric as opposed to organic, flat versus textured or shaded, negative versus positive gives students a vocabulary to use for dialogue.

Learning to see and pick out shapes in a scene or grouping of objects is an art skill that students can work on as they approach painting buildings or houses. Trying more than one way to paint the same object or scene is another art skill. One way to help children develop these skills is to provide time for them to try two approaches to painting a house — beginning with the main large shapes and working down to the details, and beginning with a small detail and working out to the details at the sides, top and bottom.

In this Expressionist painting, the primary and secondary colors stand out clearly. Notice that each color, including black and white, is placed so that it contrasts with an adjoining color, heightening the visual effect. Pick out the places in which Kirchner used pairs of contrasting colors. Notice the man's green and red face, the blue outlines around the man's body, the red, green and pink of Dodo's hat, and the red and blue outlines around her dress and body. Ernst Ludwig Kirchner, *Dodo and Her Brother*, 1908–1920. Oil on canvas, 67⅛″ x 37⁷⁄₁₆″ (170.5 cm x 94 cm). Smith College Museum of Art, Northampton, Massachusetts.

4 Emphasizing Color

Mixing new colors is part of the fun and intrigue of painting. Mixing appeals to the scientifically minded child because the results are predictable. The mixing process is very much like a laboratory experiment. Mixing also appeals to the restless youngster because the results are dramatic and immediate. Despite numerous mixing experiences, however, it is amazing that there is so little retention of basic color facts at any level. Part of the delight of painting seems to occur because mixing colors is always a bit magical.

Children enjoy mixing experiences at every grade level. Mixing colors also helps children gain appreciation of subtle color differences and associations. Basic understandings of how to make a color darker, lighter or duller and understandings about what colors clash or harmonize come from painting and mixing, too. Mixing exercises do not have to take place formally; they can happen during the course of almost any painting lesson. It is not necessary for children to remember precisely how to mix

a specific color. Instead, you can teach children how to find out what they want to know about color.

Looking at the Color Wheel

The color wheel can be thought of as the painter's reference sheet. It contains a great deal of information that is often difficult to picture correctly in one's mind. The order of the hues (the pure colors) on the color wheel comes from the order of the hues in the rainbow, or the visible spectrum. Artists found that when they placed the colors from the visible spectrum in a circle, they could see and understand the relationships between them. They were also able to make some general rules about mixing and using colors.

Primary Hues or Colors: The primary hues — red, yellow and blue — cannot be made by mixing other colors. They are primary — you have to have them to mix all the other colors on the color wheel.

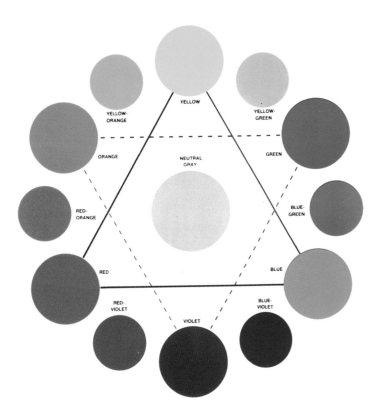

Hang a color wheel in the classroom, and point to it while discussing color combinations used in artworks or while talking about a particular grouping of colors children will be using in a painting activity. This gets children into the habit of referring to the color wheel themselves while they are working. Courtesy of Media Materials, Baltimore, Maryland.

When mixing primary colors, you may have noticed that the green you mix sometimes looks like an army green rather than a grass green. Often, the purple looks like a plum or brownish color rather than violet. That is because the primary colors are not always pure. We think of fire-engine red as a primary red. But, in fact, fire-engine red has some yellow in it, which in turn affects the secondary mixtures made with the red. What we think of as the color magenta is also considered a primary red. It is a cooler red, and, when mixed with blue, will produce a clearer violet.

We often think of royal blue as a primary blue, but royal blue actually has a touch of red mixed into it. A primary blue approaches what is considered the color turquoise. When this blue is mixed with yellow, it yields a brighter, clearer green. When mixed with a pure red, it yields a clearer violet. If this is the case, why not use magenta and turquoise as primary colors? Unfortunately, magentas and turquoises vary too. Some magentas have blue mixed into them. Some turquoise paints seem to be a bit dull.

To make the situation even more complicated, the formulas for paints differ from one paint company to another and from year to year. Paint colors are made from both natural and chemical pigments and powders suspended in a binding medium. Some of the washable paints have more binder and less pigment, which also affects how the colors behave. The implication of all this is that you really do need to take a few minutes to experiment with the primary colors to be used before introducing them to children. Introducing one set of primaries is complicated enough for elementary school children. After they have had some experience with one set of primaries, alternative reds and blues can be introduced and discussed, and children can be encouraged to expand their color-mixing experiences.

Secondary Hues or Colors: Orange, green and violet lie between the primary colors on the color wheel. Children understand that these colors are called *secondary* because they are made by mixing the primary colors together.

Intermediate, or Tertiary, Colors: These colors can be created by mixing a primary hue with a secondary color. Yellow-orange, red-violet and blue-green are examples of intermediate colors. Intermediate means *between* or *in the middle*.

Warm Colors and Cool Colors: A color can be either warm or cool, depending on how much red or blue it contains. In general, colors from yellow to red-violet on the color wheel are considered warm colors. They remind us of warm seasons, fire and sunlight and are often perceived as advancing or coming toward the viewer when used in paintings. Cool colors range from yellow-green to violet. They

This student painted half of her line drawing with warm colors, the other half with cool colors. Linda Finnegan, grade 1. Jackson Street School. Art teacher: Jacklyn Coe.

Fauves, a group of early twentieth century painters in France whose name means "wild beasts," sketched ordinary scenes but used color in expressive ways to communicate the emotional impact of these scenes. In this painting of a spooky tree, groupings of contrasting colors were used to create the dramatic shimmering effect. Fauvist tree, Carey Ascenzo, grade 6.

remind us of cool seasons and of sea and sky, and seem to recede, or fall back, when used in a painting.

Harmonious Colors: The terms *harmonious* and *contrasting* refer to the quality of color relationships. Harmonious colors are those that are related to one another or most alike one another, or are near one another on the color wheel. Red, orange and yellow form a set of harmonious colors. Harmonious colors do not dull one another when mixed.

Contrasting Colors: These colors are opposite one another on the color wheel. They are most dramatically different from one another. Red/green, orange/blue and yellow/violet are pairs of contrasting colors. When placed side by side, each set of contrasting colors produces almost a vibrating effect. But when mixed together, contrasting colors dull, gray or neutralize one another. When a hue is mixed with a little bit of a contrasting color, it lowers the intensity or brightness of the color.

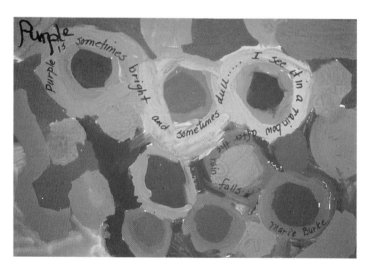

Students chose a favorite color and experimented by mixing it with every other color that was available. Notice that by mixing purple with the contrasting colors yellow and green, the intensity, or brightness, of the color was lowered. This was a combined language arts/art activity. After experiencing the impact of color mixing firsthand, children composed color poems in English class and wrote them on their paintings. Purple, Marie Burke, grade 7, Weeks Junior High School, Newton, Massachusetts.

Browns differ according to the proportion of each primary color in the mixture. Tan is made by mixing a lot of yellow with a little red and blue. Rust has more red than yellow or blue. A darker brown has more blue. White or black can be added to any of these browns to create various skin tones and other neutral colors.

Neutral Colors: When all three primaries are mixed together or when pairs of contrasting colors are mixed together, they neutralize, or cut the brightness of, one another and yield neutral grays or browns. Browns — including tan, rust and maroon — differ depending on the proportion of each primary color.

Light and Dark Colors, Tints and Shades: Adding white or black to a color changes its value. (See Chapter 5, *Value.*)

Children gain a much more concrete understanding of color concepts when they are given an opportunity to make their own color wheels.

Painting a Color Wheel

MATERIALS: Containers of yellow, red and blue paint with small spoons for dispensing colors; brushes; mixing palettes; water dishes; paper towels for blotting brushes; circular paper 12″ in diameter; small bottle caps for drawing circles, if desired.

Remind children to begin any mixing experiment by starting with the lighter color and adding only a tiny dab of the darker color. Darker colors are much stronger than lighter ones.

Water needs to be changed frequently and brushes washed and wiped thoroughly between each mixture. Any extra paint left on the brush will influence the new mixture. Using spoons to dispense paint eliminates many brush washings. Some teachers prefer to squeeze or spoon the three primary colors directly onto their students' papers, allowing children to mix secondary colors directly on their papers as well. Whichever method you choose, remember, color wheels don't have to be perfect. They are simply a learning tool.

Theoretically, all one needs are the three primary colors plus black and white to create all other colors. In fact, mixed colors depend on the particular primary colors used, and tempera colors vary. Also, secondary and intermediate hues are not necessarily created from primary hues when they are produced commercially. They may be independently created from minerals, dyes and chemicals, so a bottled green may differ from the green you can mix from the primaries. Just as painters use a wide variety of colors on their palettes, children need the full range of colors plus black and white when they are ready to go beyond color mixing exercises.

The following exercise is good for familiarizing children with the color wheel and its uses. It is also a good example of just how rich the results of mixing media in a lesson can be. Plan for two art periods if you try this lesson. The first activity focuses on collage. The second is a color mixing and painting lesson.

Paint the three primary colors in a triangle. Touching the edge of the paper with each painted circle helps make the spacing even. When working with younger children, drawing three circles by tracing around a bottle cap is an easy way to plan the placement of the colors. Be sure to wash and wipe your brush each time you change colors.

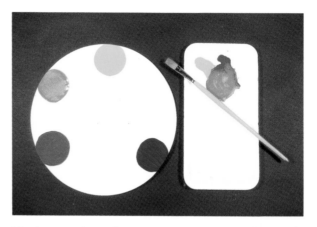

Mix the secondary colors one at a time on your palette, and paint each secondary between the appropriate primaries. Spoon a dab of the lightest color — yellow — onto your palette. Spoon a little red next to it. Mix the colors together until no streaks show. Paint the orange mixture on your color wheel. Refer to the color chart if you don't know where the color should go.

Find a new place on your palette to mix yellow and blue; spoon the colors there. Remember to begin with yellow, the lightest color, and add only a little blue at a time. You can always go back and add more to make a deeper green. Mix until no streaks show, then paint your mixture between the blue and yellow on the color wheel. Wash and wipe your brush thoroughly. Now mix red and blue together on your palette.

Have students mix the intermediate colors by varying how much of each primary they use. This requires children to concentrate on proportion and placement. These are examples of color wheels by children in grades 4 and 5. When children have finished their color wheels, they can try mixing all the colors and painting the resulting brown mixture in the middle.

Select one of the primary or secondary colors from the color wheel. Find as many different papers with mixtures of your color as you can. Cut them into geometric or freeform shapes.

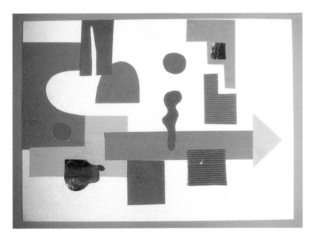

Arrange the shapes in a pleasing composition and press them onto your paper with small dots of glue around the edges and in the middle of each shape. Make some shapes touch one another, some touch the edges of the paper and some overlap. After some children are finished glueing their shapes, direct the class's attention back to the color wheel. Challenge students to choose a harmonious color and find as many tints, shades and hues of that color as they can to add to their collages. If the original color was orange, the harmonious colors would be either red or yellow.

Mixing Media: Composing a Color Collage

This two-part lesson begins by looking at the color wheel and selecting a primary or secondary color to focus on when creating a collage. Demonstrate the process by first choosing a color, such as orange. Select tints, shades and mixtures of orange from a box of papers. You might choose some red-orange papers, some peaches and some brownish-orange or tan papers, etc. Sometimes the cutoff lines between colors become confusing. That is because they are confusing. That is part of the fun of working with, and understanding, color; it is just not cut-and-dried. Does gold belong with yellow or orange? The answer is that it could probably be used by children who have selected either color. What makes this a rich learning experience is thinking about the question! If you want children to spend time looking for subtle color differences as they choose papers, don't put the glue out right away. Let children choose papers and concentrate on cutting for a few minutes first.

MATERIALS: 10″ x 16″ white drawing paper, scissors, white glue, different kinds of paper in many colors cut into 3″ or 4″ pieces (tissue paper, construction paper, sections of color from a magazine, wrapping paper, shiny paper, textured paper, corrugated paper, ribbon, colored railroad board, felt, etc.).

Mixing Media: Painting the Collage

MATERIALS: Each child needs an original color he or she has chosen, a related color and white. It is better to use individual paint cups so children have only the colors they need. Medium-size watercolor brushes such as sizes 6 to 8 work well for this assignment. You will also need water dishes, paper towels for blotting brushes and mixing palettes.

Experiment with mixtures of your colors. Try mixing the two harmonious colors. Try mixing white with each of the colors to make a pale and deep tint. Look for negative shapes within your collage and paint them in with your mixtures. Use each mixture several times to paint big and little shapes. Use your colors to add lines, textures, patterns and designs on top of your shapes. Cover the whole page with color.

Children are able to mix a wide range of hues and tints when given only limited colors to work with. By asking children to check their paintings for both pale and deep tints of each color, you can give children criteria for judging whether or not they are finished. Denise Courtney, grade 1.

Mixing Colors Optically

Colors can be mixed on a palette, then painted on paper. Colors can also be mixed directly on paper. A third way to mix colors is optically. The Impressionists and Pointillists were intrigued by the discovery that, when dots of two colors are placed close to one another, the eye perceives the painted area as a mixture of the two colors. They liked the way optically mixed colors created a shimmering effect, giving a sense of liveliness and immediacy to their paintings. Using dots also made each plane of the picture feel more varied and three-dimensional.

These artists were fascinated by the discovery that color does not leave an object just because it is in shadow. They trained themselves to see colors in shadows as well as in objects. Many Impressionists and Pointillists eliminated the color black from their palettes. Instead, they used dots of contrasting colors, as well as other colors to create the deeper colors they found in the shadows.

Practicing shading a single piece of fruit or a simple vase shape is a worthwhile exercise for older children to do before painting still-life compositions. Adding shadows to the objects in a painting creates the illusion of three dimensions on a two-dimensional surface. Shading a round shape using a pointillist approach to painting is easier than shading with a brush because children don't have to worry about the direction of their brushstrokes. One option is to present the idea of shading by using the four steps illustrated on the following page. Then, if children are developmentally ready to attempt shading, they can see a way to begin. Other children will simply disregard the whole idea.

Children can use this assignment to work realistically, as well as nonobjectively. Often, their shapes will suggest realistic subject matter. Neall Pogue, grade 1.

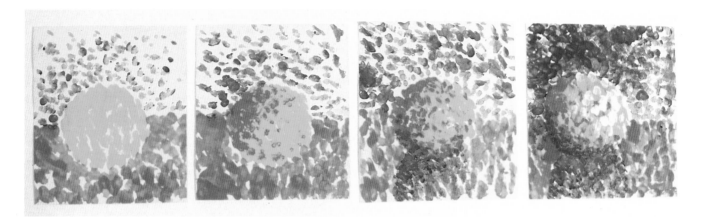

After children are set up to begin this activity, have them follow these steps: 1. Dot in a basic color and shape for the piece of fruit and the background. 2. Add dots of other colors to optically create the secondary and intermediate colors. 3. Dot in the shadows using the contrasting color. 4. Use white dots to show where light hits the piece of fruit. Dots of color in the background make the painting richer in color and more interesting.

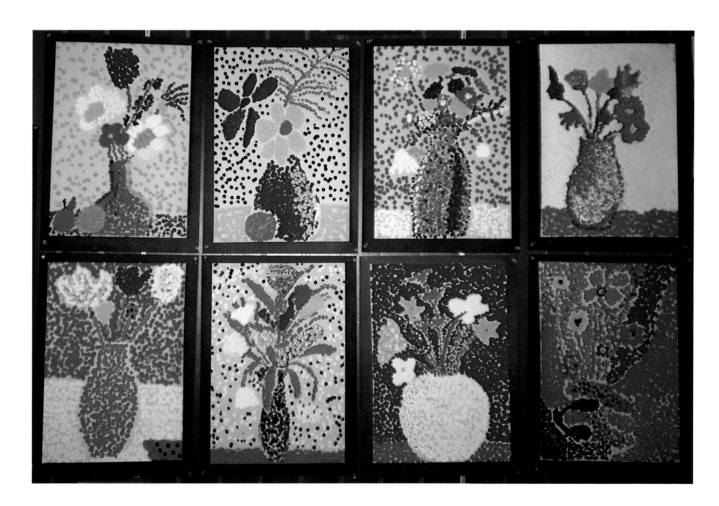

Seurat was especially interested in scientific research on the division of light into its constituent colors. He used a technique that came to be known as Pointillism, in which he broke down the colors he perceived in nature into tiny dots or brushstrokes of complementary pure hues. Colors were recombined in the eye of the spectator. Notice the contrasting areas of sunlight and shadow created by using complementary colors. Georges Seurat, *Woman with a Monkey* (study for *Sunday Afternoon on the Island of La Grande Jatte*, 1884. Oil on panel, 9¾" x 6¼" (25 cm x 16 cm). Smith College Museum of Art, Northampton, Massachusetts.

Sixth-graders created these still lifes of flowers in a vase using tempera markers and a pointillist approach.

Using a Pointillist Approach

Place a single piece of fruit on a piece of construction paper that is different from the color of the fruit. Before distributing paint, ask children to identify where light hits the fruit and to point out the shadows they see. Each child will see the light and shadows slightly differently, depending on their point of view. Keep the papers small, since painting with dots takes time. White paper works best for this exercise because it reflects the light, and because parts of the paper will not be covered by paint. Cotton-tip swabs work well for this exercise. So do tempera markers, which are small bottles of tempera paint with little, round sponges on top. Tempera markers produce larger dots than swabs, so when using them, increase the paper size.

MATERIALS: Paints in the three primary colors plus white, a set of cotton-tip swabs for each color for each child, extra swabs (since they wear out quickly), 5" x 6" pieces of white paper.

Summary

By engaging in color mixing activities, children can discover why red, yellow and blue are called the primary colors. They can learn to mix their own secondary and tertiary colors. By studying the color wheel, they can learn what color combinations are pleasing, which colors contrast with each other and which colors dull each other when mixed. Children should become familiar enough with the color wheel to use it as a reference when they are contemplating what color to choose next.

Rinsing and wiping the brush between colors is a skill that should be emphasized in this chapter. Children should also experiment with using a palette to mix colors.

Adding paint to a collage is one way to break down the picture plane as well as to add textured surfaces to paint.

5 Value

Value refers to the lightness or darkness of gray or a color. The highest or lightest value would be pure white. The lowest or darkest value would be pure black. When placed side by side, pure black and pure white yield the greatest degree of contrast possible. But, when mixed in different proportions, black and white dull one another and produce an infinite number of gray values ranging from a very pale, delicate gray to a dark, cold gray.

Young children are naturally drawn to black paint because of its power. They also enjoy experimenting with white and the many delicate pastel colors they can make by mixing white with a color. They seem to sense that black and white are different from all other colors. It helps them to think of black as the absence of all color. For instance, in the

night, when there is no light, we cannot distinguish colors at all. Black dominates everything.

By contrast, white is thought of as the presence of all colors. During the day, all colors are visible. You can show this graphically to children by letting them look at how a sunbeam of white light breaks down into a rainbow of colors when seen through a prism.

Black and white pigments, like color pigments, come from natural substances such as minerals and earth as well as from manufactured materials. Usually, black and white are included when listing colors. However, black and white are not seen in the rainbow, and they are not included on the color wheel. Black and white have different characteristics than the colors on the color wheel. When black is mixed with a color, it makes the color darker. The resulting mixture is called a *shade*. When white is mixed with a color, it makes the color lighter; the result is a *tint*. When both black and white are mixed with a color, the result is a *tone*. It is easy to remember the definition of tone if you think of the

Before painting this picture, children visited the statues of lions in the main square of the city of Reggio Emilia. They touched the lion, climbed on it, measured it, sculpted it and dramatized a lion roaring. *Portrait of a Lion,* child age 5 or 6, La Villetta School, Reggio Emilia, Italy.

expression "Tone it down." Grays, or mixtures of black and white, "tone down," lower the intensity of, or neutralize, the colors.

Making a value chart using only black and white gives children a chance to mix a wide range of values of gray and to see graphically that varying proportions makes a big difference. They will soon discover just how powerful black or, by association, any dark color is in relation to white. Be sure to save some time so that children can discuss strategies for using black paint. Help them realize just how sensitive they need to be when using black in their paintings. It is easy to add more black to make a color darker. However, it is much more difficult to make a dark color lighter. So when mixing values, start with the lighter color, and add only a little bit of the darker color at a time.

A value chart can be completed fairly quickly. It is a good warm-up exercise before going on to painting assignments in which value will be emphasized. Any subject can be painted in values of gray. Eliminating the element of color leaves children free to concentrate on form and subtle differences in value.

Painting a Value Chart

MATERIALS: Jars of black and white paint, two brushes for each child if possible — one for the white paint and one for the black. (Small plastic spoons can also be used to add the dots of black paint. This saves an enormous amount of time washing brushes. Black is difficult to wash off a brush. Larger brushes can go in the white; smaller easel brushes or watercolor brushes can be used with the black.) Also, 6" x 12" manila, gray or white paper; water dishes; paper towels. (Note: water dishes are not needed until the end of this activity, when brushes should be rinsed clean.)

Place your paper horizontally. Load your big paintbrush with a lot of white paint, and paint a blob on one side of the paper. Leave the rest of the white paint on your brush. Using another brush, place a dab of black paint next to the white blob.

Using your paintbrush with white paint, mix the black paint with the white paint that is still on your brush. Remember to turn your brush over while you mix. Keep mixing until you have a solid light gray, no streaks showing. Again, leave your light gray paint on the brush.

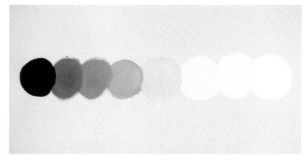

Add a new dab of black and mix it with the brush you used to mix the first gray. Mix until no streaks show. You should have a second gray that is slightly darker in value than the first. Continue adding a dab of black and mixing until no streaks are showing. Make as many different values of gray as you can. If each value touches the next one, you will be able to see the subtle differences. Try to mix at least six values of gray. End with a blob of pure black.

Ed Mell enjoys painting large vistas of the West. In this painting, the clouds seem to be moving right out of the painting and toward the viewer. Notice that the clouds almost dwarf the canyons, which are quite large. Strong, dark shades of gray and blue contrast with very light tints of gray, light blue and pure white in the sky and the clouds. Ed Mell, 1989. *Turning Clouds.* Oil on canvas, 52" x 84" (132 cm x 213 cm). Suzanne Brown Gallery, Scottsdale, Arizona. Courtesy of the artist.

When a painting is made up of many shades of color or dark values of gray, it often conveys feelings of sadness and fear. We know that we feel differently on cloudy, stormy days than on days when the sun shines brightly. Paintings with many dark and light values of gray make us also think of nighttime and the seasons fall and winter. The following activity is an effective way to practice painting skies and using values of gray.

Many elementary science units are based on a study of different kinds of clouds and the way each kind signals a different weather condition. Show a picture of wispy cirrus clouds, sometimes called "mare's tails," and explain that they are found high in the sky. Cumulus clouds are the puffy white clouds that look like cotton balls. Cumulus clouds are usually found in the middle of the sky and are always changing shapes. If you lie down on your back, you can sometimes find people, animals and mountains as you look at cumulus clouds. Stratus clouds are found low in the sky. They look like wide bands of gray and white. They warn you of possible snow flurries or drizzle. Cloud shapes are sometimes definite and sometimes not. Sometimes clouds break up into very small shapes.

Look at a variety of photographs and artists' paintings in which clouds are prominent. Point out the differences in shape and value.

Cirrus, Cumulus and Stratus clouds.

Cloudscapes in Black and White

MATERIALS: 11″ x 17″ gray paper, black and white paint, medium and small brushes, water dishes, paper towels.

Once children have made a value chart, they can use the same technique to mix tints, shades and tones of one color. This takes only a few minutes, but children are always intrigued by the dramatic results!

Using black paint, begin with a silhouette at the very bottom of the paper. You could paint a landscape or city skyline. You can include buildings, people, animals, trees, grasses, etc. Sketch in the shapes of your clouds. Touch the edges of the paper. Try overlapping cloud shapes.

Mixing Tints

Painting the sky is a good way to experiment with mixing a variety of tints, or light values of color, in a free-flowing manner. The results are usually quite beautiful. Through this exercise, children become more aware of the magnificent palette of colors that nature uses to paint the sky during different times of day. Painting skies is also a good activity to do before focusing on painting landscapes.

Begin a discussion of sky colors with the question "What color is the sky?" Eventually, children will realize that the sky can be any color. Look at paintings and pictures of the sky at sunrise, dawn, sunset, dusk and twilight. Notice the colors that the artists used in the sky and clouds. Sometimes clouds are white and puffy. At other times, they are full of different colors. Pay particular attention to the direction of the artists' brushstrokes; they tell how the clouds are moving. Look for ways in which the artists show the position of the sun.

Using white and black, fill in the sky and clouds. Use at least three values of gray — light, medium and dark. Include some areas of pure white and pure black for contrast. Matt Feinstein, grade 3.

Ask students if they think the artist of this picture painted the sky from her imagination or from observation. Georgia Pugh likes to leave interesting shapes of sky between the clouds in her paintings. Georgia Pugh, *Black Barn Green Sky,* 1985. Oil on canvas, 45" x 60" (114 cm x 152 cm). Courtesy of the artist.

The artist painted this picture after she heard that the space shuttle Challenger had exploded with all astronauts on board. Painting this sky was her way of expressing the difficult emotions she was feeling. Georgia Pugh, *Black Barn Requiem,* 1985. Oil on canvas, 45" x 60" (114 cm x 152 cm). Courtesy of the artist.

A painter of oceanscapes on the coast of Maine once gave a formula for painting skies. "Skies are easy," he said. "Just paint skies sideways and clouds up and down." This formula has proven to be an excellent introduction to blending colors directly on paper. It is also a very concrete way to teach children that the direction in which painters move their brushes makes a big difference. Children always find unique ways to expand on this workable rule.

Before you send children off to paint, ask them to close their eyes and picture the most beautiful sky they have ever seen. Ask them to remember the colors they saw in the sky and to picture the kinds of clouds.

To begin this sky painting, sweep a good amount of white paint back and forth across the paper using horizontal motions. Touch the edges and corners of the paper. Wash and wipe the brush.

Sunrises and Sunsets

MATERIALS: 11" x 17" paper; medium-size easel brushes; a good amount of white paint, smaller amounts of the primary colors; water dishes; paper towels for wiping brushes.

It sometimes makes better sense to not give children black paint the first time they try this lesson. Encourage them to use deep purple, green and blue for dark contrasts instead of black. After completing one painting of tints, they can try another painting using black as one of their colors. With black, they can create tones and shades of colors as well as tints. However, this is much more difficult because paintings get muddy easily. Night paintings or paintings of a stormy evening are good themes to suggest when adding black to children's palettes.

Begin adding colors to the sky and mixing them with the white paint to make tints. Pay attention to the direction of brushstrokes. Begin with horizontal strokes.

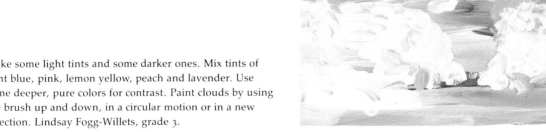

Make some light tints and some darker ones. Mix tints of light blue, pink, lemon yellow, peach and lavender. Use some deeper, pure colors for contrast. Paint clouds by using the brush up and down, in a circular motion or in a new direction. Lindsay Fogg-Willets, grade 3.

Once the paper is filled, encourage children to think about what else they might add to their sky to create contrast between light and dark areas. Sarah Izat, grade 2.

Summary

Experimenting with mixtures of black and white as well as mixtures of black and white and a color give children a chance to mix tints, shades and tones. Children learn how to make a color lighter and darker. They can use dark and light colors to suggest a particular mood, weather condition or time of day.

Children can become sensitive to the skill of using appropriate proportions of black and white when mixing. It is important to help children under-stand and verbalize the rationale for beginning with white when mixing a tint. Adding only small amounts of black at a time is also an important concept to learn when using black to make a color darker. Through these activities, children learn to mix directly on paper.

By changing the direction of their brushstrokes, painters can make one area stand out from another, such as clouds from sky. Changing directions is a painting skill children can practice and use in their own paintings of sunrises and sunsets.

Underlying this beautiful painting is a strong composition.
Looking at a painting in terms of its composition is an
intriguing exercise. Point out the horizontal line that
indicates the end of the field and the beginning of the row
of trees. That line divides the canvas into one-third field
and two-thirds trees and sky — a very pleasing proportion.
Ask students to find another place in which Monet divided
his canvas. Notice the variety of shapes and sizes of trees as
well as how they are placed. Claude Monet, *Field of Poppies,*
1890. Oil on Canvas, 23½" x 39½" (60 cm x 100 cm).
Smith College Museum of Art, Northampton,
Massachusetts.

6 Composition

The term *composition* refers to the way the art elements — lines, textures, shapes, colors and values — are arranged in an artwork. During their early years, when they engage in spontaneous art, children seem to balance their painted compositions unconsciously. However, as children grow older and more critical of their artwork, they are ready to identify and understand what it is that makes a composition pleasing. They can appreciate that creating art involves thinking, planning and using one's judgement to make decisions.

The organizing principles — rhythm, balance, variety and direction or motion — are concepts that help artists think about how art elements are arranged in a work of art. They also apply to how we arrange our living spaces or put together outfits to wear. When students are not pleased with their paintings, the organizing principles can serve as a checklist to help determine what is missing.

Working on a formally balanced painting is a concrete way to begin thinking about composition. Formal, or symmetrical, balance occurs when the same or similar elements are placed on either side of a dividing line in such a way that they form a mirror image of each other. Creating a symmetrical mask painting is a way to challenge children to formally balance a composition.

The face provides a rich structure to use as a reference. It is composed of specific features — eyes, nose, mouth, eyebrows, eyelashes, teeth, lips, nostrils, smile lines, dimples, wrinkle lines, cheeks, ears, chin, hair — that reside in specific places. Artists can take off on this format. They can exaggerate features by changing their size, shape, color or texture. A mask design grows and changes as each feature is added. That is part of the fun. Each change suggests another. Faces can turn out to be funny or scary, or simply striking in their designs. By connecting the various features with lines, the face is broken into planes, making it much easier to paint.

Symmetrical Masks

MATERIALS: 12″ x 18″ heavy white paper or oak tag; medium and small easel brushes; a variety of colors of tempera paint; large markers or crayons; rulers.

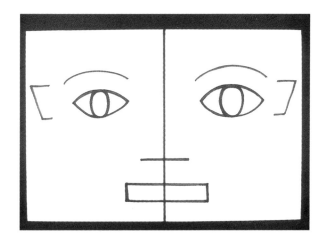

Fold the paper in half horizontally or vertically. Using a fat marker or crayon, draw the center line. (Older children can skip this last instruction, which they might find inhibiting. Younger children are more successful when they have that center line as a point of reference.) Draw the eyes, nose, mouth, eyebrows, ears and other features. Refer to the line and shape charts for ideas. Make the features big.

Look for ways to use lines to further divide up the face by connecting the features. Students should keep in mind that they are using the structure of the face to create a design.

You can influence the colors children use by varying the palette of colors for each activity. For this activity, children selected two primary colors plus black and white. They could mix any of the harmonious hues between the two primaries, or tints, shades and tones of each of the colors.

Use paint to fill in the shapes that have been created. Keep the colors symmetrical. When the base colors have dried, use a small brush to add line designs and textures. If you wish, cut out the eyes and outside shape of the mask. Add collage materials such as feathers, paper strips, yarn and sequins with white glue or staples.

Pattern and Radial Paintings

Radial paintings, pattern paintings and paintings that begin at the corners and sides — like symmetrical designs — also challenge children to pay attention to the placement of each shape, color and brushstroke.

Think about other features to add to the mask. Have hair, eyebrows, eyelashes and wrinkle lines been added?

Pattern paintings cause children to think about each mark and its placement in the picture plane. After folding the paper, make one shape or line and repeat it in each rectangle before beginning again with a new shape, line or color. Pattern painting, Brita Dempsey, age 5.

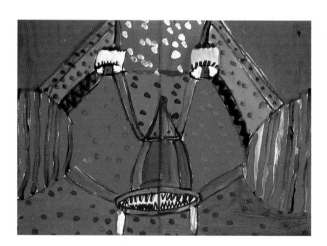

With younger students, just matching the colors so they are symmetrical is challenging enough. Mixing was not emphasized in this lesson. Ellery Brown, grade 2.

When seeing two children's paintings side by side, individual differences become clear. Children enjoy pointing out what is special about their paintings. Here, Claire filled in all the shapes with color. By contrast, Brita created her pattern from lines and textures. Pattern painting, Claire Topal, age 5.

Radial paintings are a bit more complex than symmetrical ones, since each shape or line must be placed correctly in four places instead of just two. Fold a large square of paper so you have a + or an × in the middle. Starting from the center point in each square, paint a line or shape. Turn the paper as you work repeating the line or shape in each square. Continue in the same way until the entire page is painted. Brenda Santiago, grade 2, Jackson Street School. Art Teacher: Jacklyn Coe.

During a classroom study of Mexico, children used their knowledge of myths and symbols to recreate one of the many Mexican gods. Paintings with a central motif and radiating border design provide an interesting format for children to explore when they paint shield and banner designs. Mexican sun god, Ansel Caine, grade 3.

Most art assignments and works of art are based on informal, or asymmetrical, balance. Usually, there is no center line or point. Rather, artists balance their compositions by instinctively adjusting the visual weight of the art elements. For example, a large shape in one area of the painting might be balanced by a smaller shape in another part. When any line, shape, color, texture or value is added to a painting, the artist consciously or unconsciously asks, "How will I balance this element?"

Rhythm refers to the visual flow throughout a painting — to the way one's eyes read or move through a work of art. Sometimes the elements repeat over and over in the same way, creating a pattern. Other rhythms change or grow in a regular way from one thing into another. Progressions, radiating designs, concentric and spiralling designs are all examples of patterns of growth or orderly changes.

Sometimes elements repeat, yet not in any orderly way, creating a more irregular, and often more interesting, rhythm. As students are painting, remind them to repeat their lines, shapes, textures and colors so the eye can find a pathway through their paintings. Ask, "How do my eyes move through this painting? What art elements can I follow?"

In order to avoid monotomy, and to make a painting more interesting, artists strive to achieve variety in their paintings. Instead of repeating a circle over and over, an artist might vary the placement of the circles, as well as the sizes and colors. Asking children to repeat an element in a slightly different way somewhere on the picture plane is a standard piece of art teacher advice.

To achieve a great degree of variety, an artist might use the principle of contrast, balancing the circle with a square, a dark value with a light value, a straight line with a curvy one, or a color with its complement.

Usually one element stands out or is dominant in a painting. We would refer to it as the center of interest. Sometimes, it is a shape that the artist has

Notice each of the art elements: the linear arms and legs; the round, black head shapes; the textures of the baskets and produce; and the way the artist has used equal proportions of each of the colors. Each art element is repeated throughout the composition creating a slightly different, lively rhythm — almost like the beating of drums. Painting from the Dominican Republic, D. Berteac.

Stripe Paintings

Stripe paintings are a nonthreatening way to begin experimenting with principles of composition, particularly informal balance. Children are initially asked to consider which direction their beginning stripes will go. As they progress in their paintings, they can be urged to consider the other principles of composition as well.

Many modern artists have experimented with painting canvases filled with stripes of color at some point in their careers. Some artists have chosen to dramatically vary the width of the stripes; others paint large areas of one color broken by a few slender bands of very subtle colors. Some artists paint hard-edged stripes, while others prefer stripes that appear more painterly. Many stripe paintings begin as nonobjective art — art in which the artist has no intention of painting realistic objects. Often, however, horizontal stripes begin to suggest land and sea, vertical stripes suggest masts of ships, trees, buildings and telephone poles, and diagonal stripes suggest movement. Therefore, paintings and intentions are apt to change as the artist works.

There are many ways to structure a stripe painting activity. You can keep the focus narrow by limiting the number of directions stripes may go and the number of colors available for mixing. In the following activity, students review what they have learned about color during their elementary school experience. They choose one kind of color to explore from a list: tints, shades, contrasting colors, warm or cool colors, harmonious colors, neutral colors. Instruct children to sketch out their stripes first with a piece of chalk, or encourage them to allow their compositions to unfold as they paint. Stripes can be painted on paper or on remnants of cardboard or wood. Stripes can be painted on very large or small surfaces. Stripe paintings can stand as individual paintings or can be combined to create a colorful group mural. Small stripe experiments can be glued to a larger piece of paper and used as a stimulus for a new painting or mural.

emphasized; other times, it is a subject such as a person or animal. If you ask children to close their eyes, then open them noting what they see first in a particular painting, they will often be able to point out the center of interest. Works of art are usually more interesting to look at when the center of interest is offset, not in the middle.

Often the elements in a painting are aligned in a particular direction or seem to move in a particular way. When lines or shapes are organized horizontally, they seem restful, grounded, stationary. Vertically organized elements direct the eyes upward. Compositions containing diagonals seem dynamic. Circular or spiralling movements appear to be more playful.

Choose a paper shape.

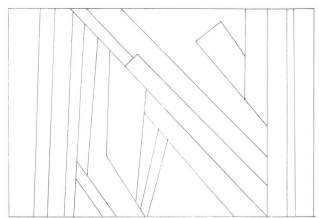

Stripes can be horizontal, vertical, diagonal or curving. Choose no more than two directions. Draw stripes with chalk. Think about varying the length and the width.

Sometimes children begin painting with one group of colors such as tints and deviate from that limitation by adding a dramatically different color such as black, resulting in a striking contrast. They seem to do this unconsciously. You can help children realize their own innate sense of color and balance by calling this to their attention. Christian Vigeland, grade 6.

Individual stripe paintings may be combined to create a striking group mural. Figuring out how paintings will be combined is a way to continue thinking about composition. Gluing a lightweight cardboard box to the back of a painting is a way of making the mural three-dimensional. Stripe paintings by sixth-graders.

This huge painting — the size of six Volkswagen Rabbits lined up — was created during a significant period in the artist's life. During this period, the artist titled his paintings after the names of ancient circular cities in Asia Minor. This painting is named for one of the gates that surround the city of Damascus. The bands of color recall structural supports such as arches. Stella was interested in color, balance and diagonal movement as he created this hard-edge, abstract painting. Frank Stella, *Damascus Gate (Variation III)*, 1969. Polymer and fluorescent polymer paint on canvas, 10' x 40' (305 cm x 1219 cm). Smith College Museum of Art, Northampton, Massachusetts. Gift of the artist.

Experimenting with Stripes

MATERIALS: Circles, half circles, rectangles, squares and triangles of paper; paint trays; water dishes; a variety of thin and thick brushes; mixing palettes; paper towels.

Thinking about the organizing principles — rhythm, balance, repetition, variety, movement, contrast and emphasis — helps individuals choose which elements they will use and how they will use them. As children work, encourage them to step back to evaluate how they are doing. Questions to ask include: "Do you need to repeat any colors for balance? Have you achieved some variety in the sizes and kinds of stripes you have used and in the colors you have mixed?" The ultimate goal is to create a harmonious, unified work of art in which the various elements hold together around a center of interest. Taste, or one's aesthetic sense, develops by practicing making decisions. It also develops by looking at and discussing ways in which other artists arrived at those decisions.

Summary

Through working with the art principles — repetition, rhythm, balance, contrast and emphasis, children become more sensitive to what makes a composition pleasing. Creating formally balanced symmetrical and radial paintings as well as informal stripe compositions gives students a chance to pay special attention to the art principles.

Just doing the painting, however, is not enough. Pointing out the ways in which each painter has achieved unity encourages children to apply their understanding and use their new art terms.

Part Two
Subjects and Themes

Flowers and still life, landscape, animals and people are all popular subjects that children often choose to paint. The following chapters place emphasis on using the art elements and principles to study and express one's impressions of a particular subject. Choose one theme at a time, and explore it in depth, adding new challenges as children are ready for more input. Try to coordinate with classroom units of study.

Spring Flowers, Emily Breines, grade 5.

Pegasus by Carolyn Dashef, 1990. Courtesy the artist.

7 Flowers and Still Life

A Vase of Flowers

Vases of colorful flowers arranged so each child has a good view are compelling subjects to paint. The different shapes and variety of hues and tints in flowers are fun to study and a challenge to mix.

When choosing flowers, try to get a variety of shapes. Arrange them so they can be seen from all points of view. Also try arranging flowers so some are high and some are low. Pull a few out so the stem and leaf lines and shapes of individual flowers are visible.

Painting a Vase of Flowers

Demonstrate planning a composition. Point out the shape of the vase and flowers together. Will that overall shape fit best on a horizontal or vertical format? Deciding which way to align the paper — vertically or horizontally — is a good beginning point for any lesson because it draws children right into the decision-making process.

Look at the shape of the vase. Discuss placing it somewhere near the bottom of the paper so there will be room for the flowers. Demonstrate using your finger or brush without paint to determine the size of the vase and the size and position of a few flowers. Use either a brush loaded with one color of paint, a piece of chalk or a fat, light-colored crayon to lay out the structure of the flower composition. These drawing tools all create bold lines and large areas that break up the picture plane. Lines and shapes created by pencils are much too finicky for most children to paint in with any degree of success. So, stay away from pencils when painting with children, and explain why you have made that decision. Sketching out the overall plan with one color will naturally help create a unified composition, since some of the sketching color will probably show as children paint in their sketches.

MATERIALS: Manila paper about 11" x 17", a tray of paints with all the colors (when working with inexperienced painters, withhold the black paint, since it can easily muddy the colors), medium easel

Direct students to paint a still life of a vase and flowers: Choose a horizontal or vertical format, whichever works best for the composition. Look at the shape of the vase, then sketch it near the bottom of the paper.

Using the same colors, sketch in the shapes of the flowers. Try for a variety of shapes and sizes in your painting. Include flowers from at least two points of view — a top, side, three-quarter or back view. Overlap one or two flowers. Let the flower shapes fill the paper; some can go off the edges.

Add stems and leaves.

brushes, mixing trays, paper towels, water dishes.

Discussing and demonstrating the process of painting in is helpful too. Mix a color and ask children to point out all the places they see that color. Paint as they respond. Point out how much easier and faster it is to paint many shapes and areas with one color before washing your brush and moving to a second color. Point out how reflecting a color in several parts of the picture helps unify the painting.

This lesson is also good for teaching children to deal with the background of their pictures as they work. Asking them to paint a little of each color they use somewhere in the background is one easy way to achieve a pleasing background effect. Students can think about placing background colors so that they bring out the subject matter. In other words, instead of placing pink near a pink flower, paint it next to a green leaf so the leaf will stand out. If students do paint a little of the background at the same time they paint the subject matter, their paintings will exist as more unified wholes. In addition, there won't be that big question of what to do with the background at the end of the lesson. When reflecting colors in the background, show students how to tone down the colors by mixing them with a little white or a little of another color. This will ensure that the background colors will be more muted than the colors in the flowers and vase in the foreground. If you are working with younger children or want to simplify the lesson, paint on colored construction paper, and don't worry about painting the background at all!

Mix a color, and paint it wherever you see it in your flowers. Paint a little of the color in the background, too.

Mix another tint, and repeat the above process. Mix several variations of each color. Paint some colors that you see and some from your imagination.

Mix several different greens — yellow-green, blue-green, forest green. Paint each color that you mix several times, and blend some into the background. Fill the paper with color. When the whole paper has been painted, go back with a small brush and add textures, small lines, dot and dab details.

This student used red paint to plan her composition. Notice that the red outlines, which are still visible, help unify and clarify some of the images in the painting. Alyssa Donaldson, grade 3.

This student concentrated on outlining one flower with black paint. He then chose one color, purple, and white and experimented with mixing gradations of a tint. This painting assignment followed the value exercises on pages 54–56. After flowers were painted, students tried the same procedure for painting the green leaves. Irises, Michael Colwell-Lafleur, grade 3.

Still-Life Compositions

Still-life compositions are traditional subjects for all painters and art students. Artists often look at a diverse grouping of objects as symbols that tell about life in a particular time and place. Grouping assorted man-made and natural objects together and arranging them until they form pleasing compositions is something artists have done for hundreds of years. Still-life arrangements can be made from machine parts, musical instruments, sports equipment, games and toys, stuffed animals, art supplies, books, bottles and vases, flowers, fruit, vegetables, office supplies, jewelry and even cooking and gardening utensils.

Choose objects of different sizes and heights. Choose some objects with patterns or designs and some that are plain. Look for some objects that have similar or related colors and some with contrasting colors. An odd number of objects is usually more pleasing than an even number. When working with younger children, arrange fewer objects and avoid wild patterns and prints, since they can be distracting. In short, the principles of art—balance, repetition, variety, movement, rhythm, contrast and emphasis—must be taken into account when arranging as well as painting a still-life composition.

If schedules allow, each child can bring in an object for the still-life arrangement. Selecting objects forces students to look at an object from an aesthetic point of view. It probably makes more sense for you to arrange several small still lifes for painting. However, if time allows, children can practice setting up their own arrangements.

When artists look at an arrangement of objects, they begin to find relationships between one object and another. Artists look beyond the flowers, vases and pieces of fruit, and see them as arrangements of shapes, lines, colors and textures. When looking at a still-life arrangement with a group of children in preparation for painting, help them see the predominant shapes in the composition and look for possible repeating art elements. It is by repeating art

Margaret chose a vertical format for her still life. She concentrated on the objects and eliminated the background. Margaret Rayno-Quirk, grade 2.

Nick chose a horizontal format and included more objects in his painting than Margaret did in hers. It looks as if he was interested in painting the background as well as the foreground objects. Nick Burk, grade 6, acrylic paint.

elements that artists create rhythms in their paintings. Identifying repeating shapes helps make sketching a plan for the still life much easier.

Sketching in the basic structure of the still life is one of the most important parts of the painting process. A successful painting depends in part on a solid structure. However, deciding where to place that first mark is probably the most difficult part of the painting process. It is also the place where many children get stuck. Help children identify a place and way to begin. One approach is for students to focus on an object that attracts their attention. Students can then add objects to the right, left, above and below their central object. They should continue adding objects until they reach the edges of their papers. Demonstrate laying out the structure of a composition with a brush and one color of paint, and comment as you work on the reasons for the way you are arranging your objects.

It helps for children to see how a still-life painting develops. Having a beginning sketch, an in-process painting with the main colors filled in and a finished example with textures, details and patterns enables children to realize that a painting emerges in stages, not all at once.

Painting in a still-life composition gives the student a chance to focus on color and color relationships. As color is added to each object, the composition changes. It is an ongoing process and an exciting one. The objects are still, but the painter is alive, and the brush is constantly moving and changing. Discourage students from painting details at this time. Painting around details is difficult and tedious. Details are much easier to add by over-painting at the end. Instead, have students concentrate on defining the shapes with color and on mixing variations of each color. Keep in mind that colors do not have to be realistic.

A few boxes draped with tablecloths, scarves or swatches of material help unify a still life setup and also enable objects to be placed at different heights.

Direct students to plan their compositions: Decide which way the objects will best fit on the picture plane. You don't have to fit all the objects onto the paper. Choose one object to begin with. Plan first with your finger or a dry brush. Keep objects fairly large. When you are ready, choose one color of paint and sketch in the shapes of the objects. Work to the edges of the paper. Overlap some objects.

Direct students to paint their compositions. Paint the negative shapes of the background first with a neutral color. This will make the overall painting procedure much easier. Painting in the background anchors the composition and enables you to see the color of the objects in relation to the color of the background as you paint. You can always add to or change the background color.

Select and mix one color at a time and paint it in several places on the composition. Continue mixing colors and painting them throughout until the paper is filled with paint. Ask children to consider how they are using their brushes as they paint. Do they wish to use special texture strokes or particular directions? In general, it is effective to follow the shape of the object with the brush.

Instruct students on how to unify their compositions: When you are finished painting in all of the shapes, you are ready for the final phase of still-life painting — stepping back to see whether the composition is unified. Students should keep in mind that they are trying to make relationships between objects. Using a small brush, they should go back and add textures, patterns, designs and details. Remind students of principles of repetition and variety.

This painting is from the same still-life grouping as the previous painting series. However, the point of view is different. Notice that the backgrounds in these two paintings of this still life are quite different. Sara wanted to paint her still life as if it were a picnic laid out on the grass. Her style seems to be especially painterly and textural, giving the painting a sense of liveliness. Sara Schiefflin, grade 4.

Summary

This chapter encourages children to apply the abstract elements and principles of art to painting realistic subject matter. Attention is drawn to each of the many decisions that have to be made in planning a composition — especially the alignment of the paper, and the initial placement and size of the vase or the first object of a still life. The skills of planning the layout with a finger or dry brush and sketching in the composition with one color are developed in this chapter as well.

Strategies for developing a painting are also emphasized. Using one color throughout a painting is a skill that helps painters give equal attention to all parts of a painting at the same time. It is part of a painterly process that artists use to achieve unified works of art. To approach a painting in this way means looking at the entire paper surface from an abstract point of view, as a composition of shapes and colors rather than just as individual objects. This way of looking goes contrary to the way most children work and think. The natural tendency seems to be to paint the vase or one tiny flower or leaf, and then rinse the brush and get a new color. Help children understand the rationale for trying out a new approach to painting. Help them realize that using one color in several places is also a way to conserve paint and get the most mileage out of each color they have mixed!

Effectively dealing with the background in a painting is also a new concept for most children. Repeating colors from the composition in the background, toning the colors down, contrasting the background with the subject and painting the background at the same time as the foreground are all artistic strategies for children to discuss and try out.

As a group of children finishes painting flowers or still-life compositions, ask them to identify unifying elements within their paintings — shapes, lines, textures or colors that repeat. This is an exciting way to study paintings from an aesthetic point of view.

8 The Environment

If you could live anywhere you wanted, where would you live? Some people want to be near a vast expanse of water. Others prefer a mountain or forest landscape. Many people thrive on the hustle and bustle of city life, while others feel most content when experiencing the subtlety and stillness of the desert. Many painters are sensitive to the environments in which they live, and their art is often influenced by those environments.

Landscape painters know that the landscape can evoke a variety of emotions, depending on the light, time of day, earth formations, weather conditions and seasons. The colors, values, shapes and textures used by painters can suggest an infinite number of moods and feelings.

To paint any landscape or waterscape, it helps to begin by thinking about the placement of the horizon line — the place where the sky meets the surface of the earth. That "line" divides the paper and gives a sense of structure to the painting. It also gives children a new perspective on the space they refer to as "air," which characteristically lies between the sky and land in young children's paintings. When children look into the distance, they will see that the sky does indeed come all the way down to meet the earth.

Ask children to estimate what proportion of their paper will be devoted to the sky and how much to the earth. Point out the proportions in other artists' paintings, commenting that the horizon line seldom lies directly in the middle of the pictures. Paintings usually have more vitality and interest when the horizon line is offset.

Painting vistas of sky and earth gives the artist an opportunity to think about ways to create the

Dunow's painting of a Mexican landscape seems to draw viewers right in — as if they were flying low over the land in a small plane. The sizes of the fields and trees get smaller and closer together in the background. Dunow divides the land into a patchwork of hills, fields and trees painted in rich warm mixtures of greens, tans and yellows. Gradually those colors change to a palette of purples, blues and blue-greens in the distant hills. Esti Dunow, *San Miguel de Allende, Mexico.* Oil on canvas, 34" x 30" (86 cm x 76 cm). Courtesy of Bowery Gallery, New York.

To create a feeling of distance in a picture, choose one object and show it in two places — close up in the foreground and far away in the background. Keep these general guidelines in mind:

Objects up close are usually big, detailed, bright, low in the picture.

Objects in the distance are usually small, indistinct, dull, high in the picture.

illusion of space and distance. Identifying foreground, middleground and background areas is a first step to understanding how to create such illusions. Present a few basic guidelines for creating distance in a work of art, then encourage children to point out instances in which artists have used such guidelines. Finally, encourage children to try out one or more principles in their own landscape paintings.

It can be intriguing to show two approaches to landscape painting. Try sketching one plan for a painting by beginning with the smallest, most distant objects in the background and working to the foreground. Or, use the same basic approach, but begin with the largest objects in the foreground and work to the background.

Another way to approach landscape painting is to consider the viewpoint of the artist. Where was the artist standing when the picture was painted?

Was the artist looking up from below, down from above or straight into the distance, or was the picture painted from an aerial, or bird's-eye viewpoint?

Each of the preceding principles can be applied to any of the following activities.

Oceanscapes

People throughout the ages have been drawn to the ocean for many reasons. The ocean nourishes and sustains us with fish and other products. It is a place where many people earn their living. The ocean links the countries of the world, and, for many hundreds of years, was the only way trade and knowledge passed from one civilization to another. For many people today, the ocean is a place to vacation and relax. For others, it is a source of inspiration.

Like our emotions, the ocean changes. Sometimes it is menacing, raging and scary. At other times, it is calm and tame. Sometimes it can seem even playful.

To get in the mood and help children recall what it feels like to be at the ocean, it is fun to play a recording of ocean sounds. Move your hand as you imagine the waves are moving. Using descriptive words, you can help children recall the soothing sounds of waves moving back and forth in a steady rhythm. Look closely at paintings of the ocean. Which painting looks like a stormy sea? Which looks like a calm sea? Point to the horizon line; notice how it tells you what kind of a sea there is.

Notice the bands in the ocean. Sometimes you can see clearly where a coral reef begins and ends because the color of the water looks different and the waves break in a specific place. The bands of the ocean can also tell you where the water is shallow or deep.

Is the ocean always blue? Notice the many colors artists have used in painting the ocean. Point out that a large expanse of water can act as a giant mirror reflecting the colors in the sky.

Painting an Oceanscape

MATERIALS: 16" x 22" paper, medium easel brushes, paper towels, trays of all different colors of paint.

This is an especially enjoyable free-painting lesson. Stop while children are working to point out unique solutions to this assignment; this will spark new ideas for other children. Comment on the colors children have used in their oceans and skies, on the different ways they have shown waves and on reflections in the water. You might also have children comment on the kind of oceans they are trying to paint. This lesson can easily be adapted for painting any kind of waterscape, especially local rivers, ponds and lakes.

Ask students to think: "Will your ocean be stormy or calm? How will you show the difference on your horizon line?" Students should each choose one color of paint and use their brushes to sketch in the horizon line. The paintings will be more interesting if they avoid placing the horizon line directly in the middle.

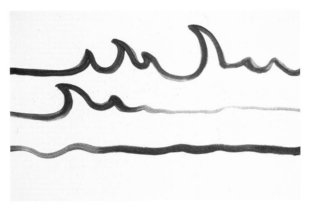

Paint lines to represent the bands of the ocean and show where waves break. These lines will help give structure to the painting.

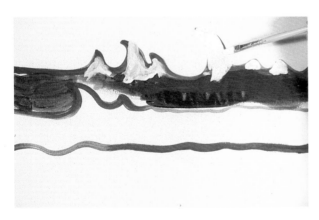

Paint in the sky and water using a horizontal direction. To show whitecaps — the foamy, white part of breaking waves — mix white into the color to make it lighter. Paint with the motion of the breaking waves.

To show the bottom of the wave or the deeper, darker parts of the water, use black or a dark color to mix shades. Remind students to paint the way the water would move. Use many different colors in the sky and ocean, and try mixing tints and shades of those colors as well.

When choosing ocean paintings to study and discuss, select those that focus exclusively on water so the emphasis is on the horizon line, bands of the ocean, movement of the waves, and colors in the sky and water. Suggesting that children can add boats, people, etc., to their paintings can come at a later time or in a follow-up painting. Alex D. Dzigurski, *Pacific Moonlight.* Oil on canvas. Collection of Dr. and Mrs. Philip A. Weisman.

You might show a giant wave or waves breaking against a rocky shore. James Egelhofer, grade 2.

The colors an artist puts into a sky tells the time of day it is in that painting. Alexandra Bloom, grade 2.

Landscapes

Why do you think so many artists have chosen the outdoors as a subject for painting? When you ask children this question, you cause them to think about what subjects motivate an artist. It also encourages children to begin thinking about, and visualizing, their own landscapes.

Many artists choose to live and paint in the country, the woods, the desert or near a mountain range, where there is space for a person to see far into the distance. Being far away from the fast, hectic life of the city and suburbs, the artist can slow down, be more peaceful and have time to look, think and focus on nature.

Artists like to paint the colors they see in the land — rich greens, browns and golds of fields; colors of crops as they ripen, colors of trees in the spring, fall, winter or summer. In the country, artists can often see a wide expanse of clouds and sky and can watch colors change with the weather and time of day. In each section of our country — in the North, South, East and West — the colors in the sky and land are markedly different.

Other artists are intrigued by the way the countryside often has a sense of order about it. Large expanses of land are divided into fields of different shapes. Shapes are patterned with different line configurations, depending on which crops are planted. Some children have seen this from an airplane. Land formations such as hills, mountains, valleys and plains are distinctive in different sections of the United States and in different parts of the world.

Some artists enjoy painting scenes exactly as they look; they use naturalistic colors. Other artists believe the land can reflect a person's mood or frame of mind; they like to paint the countryside the way it makes them feel and often use more imaginative colors.

In order to paint a countryside scene, a painter looks at that scene in an artistic way. A painter analyzes the scene for its shapes or areas. It is impor-

Coffaro is known for the intense colors he uses in landscapes of the New Mexican desert. He used to be afraid of color, so he painted only with earth tones. "Then I had an awakening . . . I woke up to the fact that I could do whatever I like." He says, "I like color . . . There's no black in my palette, but magenta is in every piece I do. And red — I like red." Patrick Coffaro, *It's Warm, It's Inviting*, 1988. Chine collé, 30" x 22" (76 cm x 56 cm). Suzanne Brown Gallery, Scottsdale, Arizona. Courtesy of the artist.

tant to tell children that, in planning their compositions, they should first think about the big divisions of the land. This is not a time to add small details like people, animals, trees, fences and flowers, etc. Remind them how difficult it is to paint around small details. After they get their compositions laid out and the large areas painted in, they can go back and add smaller details on top.

This structured approach will work for most children. However, some children will insist on putting in details or approaching the theme in different ways. Often it is the gifted child who has a unique way of solving a problem. You can remind children of the rationale behind instructions, but if a child has a specific idea in mind, let that child go ahead and try out the idea. Watching what children do after we give suggestions is one of the most interesting aspects of teaching. It is really how we as teachers learn, change, grow and improve.

Direct students to sketch their compositions: Decide how you will hold the paper — vertically or horizontally. Decide on your point of view. Are you looking up into hills or mountains, down into a valley or straight into the distance? Or, do you have a bird's-eye view of the land below you? Using one color, paint the horizon line toward the top of the paper. It will make the picture more interesting if you off-set the horizon line. If you are doing a

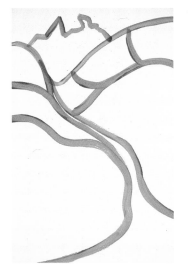

bird's-eye view, you might not see the sky, so go onto the next step.

Using the same color, divide the land into fields, desert, forest areas, mountains and pastures. If you want a road, pathway or stream in your picture, put it in now. If you wish to show hills or mountains in the distance, put them in now. Fields that are close to you should appear to be bigger, while those in the distance should appear smaller and higher up in the picture.

Painting a Landscape

MATERIALS: 16″ x 22″ manila paper, medium easel brushes, trays filled with all of the basic paint colors, water dishes, paper towels.

Encourage children to look at their paintings from a distance by asking follow-up questions: "What was the artist's point of view in this painting? How do you know? How did the artist show distance? What time of day is it in this painting? What emotions does the artist cause us to feel when looking at this landscape? What kind of colors did the artist use — imaginative or realistic? Which artists used a lot of texture in their paintings?

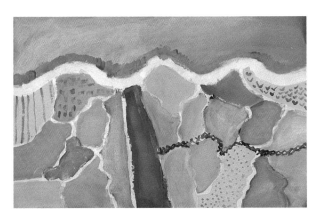

Direct students to paint their compositions: Fill in the fields and sky with areas of color. Each time you use a color, paint it somewhere else in your painting. This will save time, and it will also help unify your painting. Mix colors directly on the paper by blending one color into another. Rinse and blot your brush before going into a new color so your paint doesn't get too watery. Elizabeth Berger, grade 3.

Direct students to paint textures: Use a small brush and a variety of brushstrokes to show what kinds of crops or trees are growing in each field. Think about how you might show corn, wheat, cucumbers, pumpkins and squash. By changing the direction and length of your brushstrokes, you can make one field stand out from another. Paint textures right on top of the flat areas of color. Laura Skibiski, grade 3.

Raising children's awareness of the variety of shapes in building and rooftop silhouettes is important for the success of this activity.

Cityscapes

Ask students, "How is the city different from the country? (Noise, traffic, buildings close together, smog, pavement, many man-made shapes.) When you think about traveling to a big city, what emotions do you feel? (Excitement, energy.) What do you picture in your mind when you think of the city? (Tall buildings, grand bridges, neon lights, many people, signs, cars, taxis, buses.)" Each of us thinks about the city in a different way. Find several paintings and photographs of the city, and ask students, "What aspect of city life do the artists of these paintings show us in their pictures?"

Look at the horizon line in several paintings, drawings or photos of the city. Notice the geometric shapes and silhouettes of buildings against the sky. When we speak of the place where the sky meets the buildings and structures of the city, instead of using the term *horizon line,* we call it the *skyline* of the city. Sometimes the silhouettes of specific buildings, bridges and landmarks help us differentiate one city from another.

Many children enjoy beginning their compositions by painting the skyline in the background high on the picture plane. Other children find it is easier to begin with the stores and restaurants in the foreground and add the skyline in the background.

Goodwin was one of the few American painters to concentrate on cityscapes around the turn of the twentieth century. He would set up his old easel — and umbrella, if need be — to capture his impressions of the city from different points of view, at various times of day, during all kinds of weather. Arthur Clifton Goodwin, *New York at Night.* Oil on canvas. 29½" x 36" (75 cm x 91 cm). Courtesy of Vose Gallery, Boston, Massachusetts, and DeVille Gallery, Los Angeles, California.

Painting a Cityscape

MATERIALS: Large manila paper, medium easel brushes, paper towels, water dishes, trays of all the colors of paint.

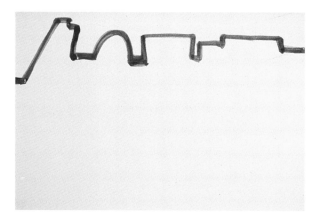

Ask students to picture themselves riding into the city or looking up at the skyline: What kinds of buildings do you see? Using one color, paint the shapes of the buildings in your skyline. Place the skyline high up on your picture plane so you have room for the buildings in the foreground. Be sure to create interest by varying the height and shapes of buildings. Are there any landmarks you want to include — any skyscrapers, cathedrals, factories, stores or offices?

You may wish to include more than one skyline to show the layers of buildings in a crowded city. Paint a street low in the picture plane. Include a close-up view of specific storefronts you would find in a city — restaurants, department stores, banks, office buildings, art museums, bakeries, repair shops and churches.

Paint in the sky and the main large shapes.

Add fire escapes, chimneys, a TV antenna, signs, traffic lights, people, trees, cars, buses, taxis and windows using a small brush. The details will add texture and interest to the city composition and will probably help give it a sense of rhythm as well. Molly Lindsay, grade 3.

Summary

WATERSCAPES: In order to begin painting a waterscape, children need to consider the placement of the horizon line and the proportion of sky to water. Recalling the recurring motions of a body of water and being sensitive to differences in the water when it is stormy or calm are important concepts for the painter to think about as well. Even a short movement activity, such as moving one's arm as one recalls waves moving, helps children internalize and use a kinesthetic response to a waterscape project. Children must also think about the time of day, weather, how they will differentiate sky from water and how they will reflect colors of the sky in the water.

Using the direction of the brushstrokes to show motion is a key concept to stress, as is the many different colors of water and sky.

LANDSCAPES: Some landscape painters begin with the sky, then add the land. They work from the background to the foreground. Other painters like to begin with the horizon line and lay out the main shapes or divisions of land. Children should be encouraged to discuss how they began their paintings and how they went about developing them.

Landscape painters reflect a variety of interests in their work. Some are interested in how land changes at different times of day and in different seasons. Others are interested in the details, textures and subtle color differences they perceive. Many artists enjoy showing the people, buildings and wildlife they see in a particular setting. Still others enjoy looking at land forms from an abstract point of view. Often artists enjoy painting with imaginative rather than realistic colors. As children look at landscape paintings by famous artists and by one another, they can identify the interests of the painters. They can also figure out the points of view of the artists.

CITYSCAPES: When thinking about cityscapes, the artist is asked to look at the shape of the skyline and figure out how and where to place it on the picture plane. The artist can start in the foreground with a close-up view of city life and move toward the background while working. Or the artist can begin with the skyline in the background as it is silhouetted against the sky and work down toward the foreground. Each strategy calls for a different kind of planning.

Painting in big areas of buildings, streets and skies before moving to small details is important to stress.

Think about including a bridge or overpass while planning a painting of the city. Joshua Levin, grade 3.

In this impressionistic collage of the city, students cut out paper and cardboard shapes of the city — especially traffic signs, lights and billboard shapes. Then they added more shapes and details with paint. James Egelhofer, grade 3.

9 Animals

After spending time watching unguided young children paint animals, it is evident that children generally use one of the following approaches.

Sometimes children break the animals down into shapes. They usually begin with an oval for the body, then add other outlined shapes for the neck, head and legs. Finally, they use lines to add details such as antlers, tusks, tails, whiskers, horns and specific markings such as dots and stripes. Children seem to use this **"shape" approach** to animals when

Amason grew up on Kodiak Island, which is known as the brown bear capital of the world. He remembers watching bear cubs sliding down mountain snowfields and fishing in rivers. Notice his brushstrokes in this painting. They begin very small as they describe the curve of the bear's snout. They grow bigger and freer as they arch over the bear's brow and continue to describe the bear's fur on his upper body. The colors in the background and the bear itself are alike. How did the artist make the bear stand out from the background? Alvin Amason, *Pretty One*. Mixed media, 66" wide x 60" high x 15" deep (168 cm x 152 cm x 38 cm). Collection of Brown and Baine, Phoenix, Arizona. Transparency courtesy of Suzanne Brown Gallery, Scottsdale, Arizona. Photographer: Charles Backus.

they do not have a specific animal to study and are relying on memory.

At other times, children begin with a blob of paint, pushing it out until it suggests the gesture or position and shape of an animal. Animals painted with a **gesture approach** seem to occur by chance as children are painting freely at the easel.

When children have a specific animal in front of them, or when they have had experience with a specific animal, they often choose a **contour approach.** As they paint the outline of the animal model or photo, they tend to be more sensitive to subtle features, and their brush drawings tend to be more accurate.

When texture is the most compelling feature, children often choose a **textural approach** to painting animals.

Any of these approaches requires sophisticated ways of analyzing the shapes and characteristics of animals and of portraying them on two-dimensional surfaces. Children are naturally sensitive to visual elements, but such skills are not usually cultivated, discussed or rewarded, so most children are not aware of what they have achieved when they draw or paint animals.

We as teachers can call attention to the fact that there are many ways to paint animals. We can ask children to verbalize how each of the approaches is different and ask them to think about the merits of each. By presenting several approaches and requiring children to test them in a rather scientific, experimental way, we give children a chance to expand their painting options. We help children cultivate skill in painting by helping them find an approach or combination of approaches that works for them. All approaches can be geared to capturing the positions and personalities of particular animals.

Children, like other artists, find animals a delightful subject for painting, but not an easy or simple subject. It is difficult to remember animals in a vacuum; it makes sense to coordinate animal paintings with classroom studies of particular animals and their habitats. One way to help children distinguish the unique shapes, features and markings of different animals is to have visuals or models available. Kindergartens and younger grades often have assorted model animals, and plastic, rubber and wooden animals are commercially available fairly inexpensively. Many children collect horses, dinosaurs or farm animals and enjoy bringing them to school for a few days. Parents, teachers and children are happy to save magazines and calendars if they are aware that a teacher is trying to gather visual resources for the classroom.

Children are always surprised by their ability to paint animals fairly accurately and charmingly when experimenting with the following brush drawing approaches. The brush is a terrific drawing tool. Children are able to work much faster, larger and more freely than they would if they were drawing with a different tool. Some children prefer medium-size watercolor brushes for brush drawing. The bristles are softer and more responsive than easel brushes, and they form a point at the end. These brush characteristics enable children to capture even the subtle details of specific animals. Other children find it easier to use stiff easel brushes. It is fun to try the same exercise with two kinds of brushes to see which works best for particular children. When preparing paint for brush drawing, make sure the consistency of the paint is fairly thin so brushes can flow easily.

The following exercises don't take long, so encourage children to try the four approaches on more than one animal. While children are working, emphasize that practice is the way to improve painting skills. Remind children that they are experimenting and that it is okay to make mistakes. In fact, tell them that, if they don't make mistakes, they probably aren't challenging themselves to try something new.

As children are about to begin choosing animals to paint, encourage them to think about the specific body shapes, features and characteristics that make their animals unique among all other animals. Giraffes have long necks, long legs and squarish bodies; they have oddly shaped markings, horns and ears. Rabbits have soft, furry, rounded bodies and heads, whiskers and long, oval ears; they have strong back legs for jumping. Lizards have long bodies with long, triangular heads and pointed tails; their skin is scaley and textured, and they have long toes.

Children should begin by looking at their animals from a side view. Usually the main features are most clearly visible from the side. Demonstrating the four approaches and simply asking children to try out more than one approach for each animal is a good strategy when time is limited. When finished, children should ask themselves which approach or combination of approaches best captures the position and personality of their particular animals.

Four Different Approaches

MATERIALS: Jars of black paint, medium watercolor or easel brushes, large sheets of newsprint, model animals or animal pictures.

Shape approach to painting animals — Feel the shape of your animal with your eyes closed. Begin with an oval for the body. Add the head, neck, legs, tail, ears, horns, whiskers. etc.

Gesture or blob approach — Hold the animal up to the light and look at its silhouette, or overall shape. Begin with a blob and work the brush out to create a solid animal silhouette. Try to capture the position of the animal.

Outline or contour approach — Begin at the top of the animal's head. Look closely at the animal in front of you. Let your brush record each detail as it moves around the animal's body.

Texture approach — Begin with the animal's features: eyes, nose, mouth and ears. Then try to convey the texture of the animal by repeating the line and shape markings you see. This approach only works with animals that have distinctive markings or long fur.

Brush sketches of a leopard and hippopotamus. David Barowsky, grade 5.

In order to reinforce the idea that practicing is a way to improve painting skills, encourage children to continue experimenting. Change the focus slightly by pointing out that animals can be painted from different points of view. Hold up an animal and ask what can and cannot be seen from front, back, side, top and three-quarter points of view. Ask children to complete brush drawings of one animal from at least three different points of view.

Encourage children to hold their animals and feel the shapes with their eyes closed. It is easier to get a good perspective and paint a large animal when standing up.

Different Points of View

Front view.

Top view.

Side view.

Three-quarter view.

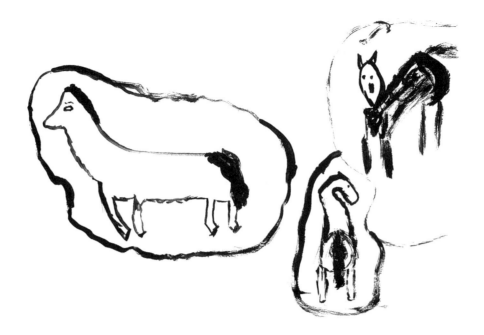

Quick sketches of a horse
from three points of view.
Thalia Brown, grade 5.

After completing animal experiments on large sheets of newsprint, children are ready to use their new skills. Younger children can concentrate on painting one large animal. In this case the emphasis should be on including all the specific characteristics of that animal. Older children can focus on composition and including several animals from different points of view. In both cases, it is important for children to add a few black lines to indicate the shape of the land forms in the background. Are there hills, mountains, trees, a fence, a barn, a river? At least encourage children to draw in the horizon line. These black background lines will help unify the composition and break the background into specific areas to paint. Without the black guidelines, children are sometimes at a loss as to where to begin.

Hand out neutral colors of construction paper such as gray, tan and brown for final compositions. Working on colored paper eliminates the need to paint the entire background and enables the beauty of the brush-drawn lines to remain evident. Make available white paint and a few other earth colors such as rust, gold, brown and gray to paint in some areas of the composition.

Working with a limited palette of earth tones or neutral colors has proven to be an effective way to achieve pleasing, unified animal compositions. Earth tones refer to the colors that come from the ground — tan, gold, rust, black, gray, beige and white. Earth tones are not found on the color wheel. They can be made by mixing all three primaries in different proportions plus black and white. Earth colors look good together, and children enjoy experimenting with this unusual palette. After all, earth colors were the original palette of the cave painters, who painted animals on cave walls so many thousands of years ago. When using earth colors, challenge children to come up with new and unusual ways to paint the sky.

Compositions in Earth Tones

MATERIALS: Tan, gold, rust, gray, brown, black and white paints; easel brushes and other small brushes for details and textures; water dishes; paper towels.

Use black paint and a medium size brush to sketch one large animal or several animals from different points of view. Before painting in with earth tones, sketch in a background that shows where your animal lives — in the woods, near water, on a farm, at the circus. Ansel Caine, grade 3.

The direction in which students use their brushes can help give paintings a feeling of movement. Britt Harlow, grade 3.

The animals children paint are often very expressive. Dan Whitlock, grade 3.

Another way to give children a chance to use their animal painting experiences is to display a large piece of mural paper. As children finish their individual paintings, they can go to the mural to work on a large variation of the individual assignment. Direct children to paint large animals in the foreground and smaller animals higher up in the background. Sometimes drawing in a horizon line and a few hills or background details will help children place their animals.

Children worked on this animal mural when they were finished with their individual compositions. At first, only black paint was available. When it was obvious that children needed a little more input, white and brown paints were also made available.

This mural was the culmination of a long study of tigers. Children looked at, pantomimed, drew and painted individual compositions of tigers roaring. They also studied, drew and painted stripe patterns. They learned about the concept of camouflage and experimented with mixing variations of orange and gold. The children decided to paint this giant mural so everyone else in the school could see what they had learned. Tiger mural by a small group of children ages 5 and 6 from the Anna Frank School — an early childhood school — in Reggio Emilia, Italy.

A Gallery of Animal Paintings

As children gain confidence in their ability to paint animals and work with paint, let them try using the full range of colors. Remind them that it is more difficult to create a unified painting when using all the colors. It helps to remember to repeat colors while they are on the brush and to work the whole paper constantly. Children characteristically focus on getting one part of the painting, such as the animal, just right before going on to the next part. The trouble with this approach is that it is very difficult to create a harmonious painting.

Rhinoceros, Alex Batten, grade 5.

Paint dark textures on top of light areas, and light textures on top of dark areas. Hippopotamus, Nick Burk, grade 6.

This is a spontaneous painting that a child did on her own. It affirms the point that times should be provided during which students can choose paint, brushes, techniques, and subjects on their own, drawing from previously learned techniques. Nina Wheeler-Chalfin, grade 3.

Dragons

The previous animal painting activities stressed keen observation. Painting dragons taps children's imaginations. In order to motivate children to paint a dragon, it is important to paint a vivid word picture, describing as many specific features, habits and details about dwelling places as possible. The dragon is an imaginary creature that has appeared in the legends of both Eastern and Western civilizations from ancient to modern times. Interpretations vary greatly. A painting activity based on dragons is an excellent follow-up to a literature unit on dragons and other creatures of the imagination.

Without letting on that the subject for this painting activity is dragons, ask students to close their eyes and use their imaginations to paint a picture in their minds as you paint a verbal picture: "Picture in your mind a creature with a serpentine, or snake-like, body and a very long, barbed tail that thrashes back and forth. This creature's body is protected by an armor of overlapping scales. It has rows of extremely sharp teeth and eagle-like claws for cutting and tearing. Some of these creatures

have more than one head. They breathe fire and emit clouds of poisonous smoke from their nostrils. Many have bat-like wings and horns. These creatures are known for their keen, penetrating eyesight, for their wisdom and for their power. What kind of creature did you picture in your mind?"

Ask children to list specific features that might be found on a dragon. Share some of the following information about dragons so children can think about the kind of dragon they wish to portray and where that dragon will live.

Dragons dwell in folklore, generally in places civilization has not yet reached. They serve as explanations for that which humankind fears or does not understand. Dragons have been blamed for stealing lost children, strayed cattle and lost treasure. As populations and civilizations have grown, dragons have ceased to be as plentiful. Also, many dragons have been slain by heroes to save damsels or populations in distress. Sometimes they have been killed for their blood, which, though poisonous, is often a vital ingredient in cures or magic potions.

In some legends, dragons inhabit the heavens, guarding the mansions of the gods. They control the

Belinda Zucker, *Dragon Painting*, 1990. Courtesy of the artist.

as basically benevolent creatures. They are associated with the powerful elements of nature. The breath from dragons' nostrils is said to form the clouds, and the pressure of their feet is thought to produce rain. Storms are caused when dragons became playful or irritated and begin turning somersaults in the air. Dragons of the Far East are very rich and wise. Philosophers have often sought their counsel, which is why dragons are usually shown holding a pearl, a symbol of wisdom. Many noble families have claimed to be descended from dragons, and the emperors of China have been called dragons. They sat on dragon thrones, rode in dragon boats and slept in dragon beds. The emperor's dragon was distinguished from other dragons by its five claws. Other dragons have three or four claws.

wind, clouds and rain. Some dragons live in the water and regulate the course of the rivers. They cause or prevent rivers from flowing to the sea. Wherever there are caves or vast mountain ranges, there are likely to be dragons. Dragons especially like caves that are close to town so they are near to a source of food. These dragons often guard ancient treasures. In the winter, dragons have been known to hibernate deep down in lakes and rivers. During the spring thaw, they ascend in a spiral pathway to the sky.

Dragons are believed to have been born out of chaos at the dawn of creation. They are viewed differently in the East than in the West. Western dragons are dreaded foes of humankind and symbols of all that is evil. They bring destruction, starvation and plagues. Slaying a dragon, and thereby ridding the world of evil, was the crowning achievement of legendary heroes such as Arthur and Beowulf. However, even the most terrifying beasts often have a sentimental side, and Western dragons have been known to be susceptible to falling in love with beautiful young maidens.

In the folklore of the Far East, dragons are seen

One way to paint a dragon is to use light ink to sketch the nose, then the eyes, mouth, fangs, mane, horns, smoke and fire. Watercolors can be used to fill in. Remember to leave some parts — such as the fangs and whites of the eyes — white for contrast. Belinda Zucker, *Dragon Painting*, 1990. Courtesy of the artist.

Painting Dragons: Shape, Features and Colors

MATERIALS: 16″ x 22″ white paper, several colors of paint (but not black), medium-size brushes.

Ask students, "Think, will your dragon be friendly or scary?" Direct them to hold their papers either horizontally or vertically, depending on which way they position their dragons. They should choose a main body shape and fill it in. It's helpful to display a variety of body shapes, as it helps children make the first mark on what can be an intimidating piece of blank paper.

Add body parts such as the head, jaws, legs, wings and tail, and paint them in. Outline and paint in each body part as it is added, or use the blob method to make the shapes.

Add other body features such as claws, teeth, a mane, nostrils, horns, fire and smoke.

Painting Dragons: Textures

MATERIALS: Black paint, small brushes, dragon paintings.

Repeat at least three of the following lines to create textures on the dragon's body: hatch, crosshatch, stipple, curvy, swirled, V'd, jagged, horizontal.

Tim Crosby, grade 5.

Jocelyn Kennedy, grade 2.

Dragon mural.

A delightful mural can be assembled easily by arranging children's finished and cut-out dragons. Dragons can be placed in particular habitats — among clouds, lurking about mountains, peeking out of caves and in, around and under lakes, rivers and swamps — or they can simply be overlapped.

Summary

ANIMALS: Different animals and circumstances influence how children go about beginning paintings of animals. In this chapter, children are encouraged to try out the blob, shape, outline and texture approaches. They are also encouraged to paint animals from several points of view — front, back, top, side, three-quarter. In other words, children are presented with a variety of strategies for analyzing animals. They are then encouraged to practice and develop several different looking and painting skills.

As they paint, children can focus on the position, distinctive characteristics, personality and environment of an animal. They will discover that the brush is an excellent drawing tool. It is quick, responsive and freer than a pencil or pen. It also forces the artist to work with bigger strokes.

Working with a limited palette of earth tones or neutral colors is a different experience for children. They should discuss whether or not they enjoyed working with this particular palette and why they think you chose to limit the palette to these colors. Painting successful animal pictures is unusually difficult when all colors are available for children to use. Often the brown rabbit gets lost in the brown hole, or the brown horse disappears when the child paints in the brown ground, and the viewer cannot differentiate anything. Presenting earth tones — or various browns — presents new options to children. Once they have succeeded in portraying animal positions and in painting them in using earth tones, they can try using the whole range of colors.

DRAGONS: Rather than using observational skills to depict animals, painting dragons asks children to use their imaginations. By verbally describing parts and characteristics of dragons and asking children to build dragons from individual parts, children can invent their own animals. They can begin from the nose and other features on the face and head, or they can begin with the shape of the body.

10 People

After painting animals, it is easy to move directly into painting people. The shape, contour and gesture approaches used to capture the spirit and feeling of animals can also be used when learning to paint pictures of people. Painting profiles as well as three-quarter, back and front views gives children a challenging yet fairly easy way to practice painting people, as was the case when they examined animals from different points of view. Beginning simply, with just black paint, places the emphasis on looking closely for position and details and on thinking about the placement of the figure on the page. Demonstrate the following three techniques so children can get an idea of the process.

Students painting portraits, grade 3.

Nick Quijano Torres, *Memories of the Veteran*, 1984. Lacquered watercolor on paper, 12½″ x 12″ (32 cm x 31 cm). From the permanent collection of the Museum of Folk Art, New York. Gift of Dorothy and Leo Rabkin.

Working from a Model

It is fun to spend a class period drawing from models. If possible, ask children to wear clothing with interesting details or patterns on the day you intend to do this lesson. Let children take turns posing for one another. Musical instruments, sports equipment, a cane, apple, tea cup, umbrella, book, telephone, spoon and bowl, bouquet of flowers and other props can generate ideas for poses. Try to make the poses interesting to children in all parts of the room. Be sure each section of the room gets an opportunity to practice painting from a few different points of view. If space is limited, some children can use drawing boards and others can work on the floor.

Keep in mind that children are self-conscious about looking at one another. Be prepared for giggles and embarrassed remarks. Acknowledge that modeling for classmates can be uncomfortable. Set guidelines for behavior beforehand. Show paintings by Pablo Picasso, Henri Matisse and other artists in which figures appear a bit distorted. That way, children can compare themselves to great artists when trying out brush painting techniques.

If children are asked to identify and move each joint in their body, beginning with the neck, they will see that they can break the body down into oval shapes. Looking at a mannequin is a way to illustrate this point dramatically.

If time is short, you can pose. This actually gives you an excellent vantage point from which to observe the children. One or two chairs placed next to a small table draped with an interesting cloth and decorated with a bowl of fruit or flowers is a classic setup. A painting or poster can be placed in the background. Of course, it is always fun to come up with unusual setups.

Instruct children to look at the head of the model and start at the top of the paper when beginning their brush drawings. Try a shape, a contour and a gesture brush drawing of one pose. This is a way to warm up and get a sense of the proportion and position of the model, as well as a way to practice. Often it is easier to stand while painting from a model. That way, children can have a better overall view of their papers, and their arms can move more freely. Progress from drawing a few short poses on newspaper or newsprint to longer, more detailed poses on white, manila or colored construction paper. Save time for children to complete brush-drawn compositions using a combination of techniques. Children should add patterns on clothing and other interesting details and should put their models into a setting. Asking children to bring their compositions out to the edges of the papers encourages them to think about the entire paper space. These black and white brush paintings may be left as they are or, once they have dried, color can be added with oil pastels (remember to use a thick layer of newspaper padding) or paint.

When children are ready to paint in their sketches, they will need a few suggestions for how to mix a skin tone. Skin tones are variations of brown (the three primary colors mixed together; they can be mixed just like earth colors). Adding brown to white is a good place to begin. If you want a warmer glow, add some yellow. For a darker skin tone, add a bit of blue or black. For a redder skin tone, add a little bit of red. For a pale, peachy complexion, start with white paint and add a little bit of orange; if it still looks too orange, tone it down with just a touch of its complement, blue. To make the

Try the shape method of painting a person. Begin with an oval shape for the head. Use ovals or circles to represent each body part. Try to capture the position of the model. Claire Topal, grade 6.

Use a contour or outline to paint the model's position. Follow the outer edge or outline of the model. Begin with the head and move slowly to the neck, shoulder and arm. Keep your eye on the part you are painting. If you need to look at your paper, stop painting and reposition your hand and brush before beginning again.

Try the blob or gesture method of painting a person. Let your arm keep moving the paint around as you get a feel for the position of the model. Keep your eyes on the model as much as possible.

peachy color warmer in feeling, add a little bit of yellow. Remember that a very little bit of another color will dramatically change light colors. Suggest that children mix enough paint to fill in all the skin at once, since mixing the exact color again would be almost impossible to do. However, if a child does run out of paint, you can point out that nobody's skin is all the same color. It is often darker on places that are exposed to the sun. It is often lighter on the palms of the hands and soles of the feet. Point out through examples of other artists' work that colors may be realistic or more impressionistic and fanciful. (See Ernst Ludwig Kirchner's painting, *Dodo and Her Brother*, page 42.)

Caution children to stay away from wet black paint as they add other colors. Begin by painting in the larger shapes of the composition and working in the drier areas. Demonstrate and remind children that painting in background areas early makes it easier to paint in the rest of the composition. Suggest a tint or neutral color for the background. As colors are added, remind children to repeat them in other areas of their compositions.

It is fun to paint from a model. Props help make models feel more comfortable and their poses more interesting.

When painting from a longer pose, students should take time to think about how the figure fits onto the page. They may add a second figure to their compositions, if they like. Direct students to look at other members of the class. They should try to include a side, back or three-quarter view and as many details as possible. Also, they should add background objects and extend their brush sketches to the sides of their papers.

Paint in the brush drawing. Repeat colors to unify the painting.

After the main colors have been blocked in, use a small brush to add textures, patterns and details. Alethia Donohue, grade 6.

Each child has an individual style. This work was also painted from the model on the left. Sara Rundquist, grade 4.

Focusing on Heads and Faces

When painting heads and upper bodies, the emphasis is a little different from painting whole figures. More attention needs to be placed on individual features and proportions of the face. Beginning a study of the face by having students focus on their own eyes helps ease a bit of the embarrassment that often accompanies any lesson in which children are asked to model for one another. Painting eyes is an especially good way to study one feature in depth. It is helpful to have small mirrors so children can study themselves. However, the same results may be achieved by looking closely at the eyes of a partner.

Nate Hulley, grade 5.

Looking Closely at the Eye

Name each part of the eye as you describe its function. When we say that someone has blue, green, brown or hazel eyes, we are talking about the iris. Have students check the color of the irises in their partner's eyes. Next, ask them to focus on the pupils in the very center of the irises; this is the part that regulates how much light enters the eye. When there is plenty of light by which to see, the pupil contracts and looks like a tiny black dot. When light is dim, the pupil opens to let in as much light as possible, and the black dot becomes much larger. That is why it takes a few moments to be able to see when lights are turned off at night or when entering a dark room after being outside; the pupil needs time to adjust.

Invite children to try an experiment with you. Ask them to close their eyes for a moment, count to twenty, then quickly open their eyes and look at one of their partner's pupils. They should be able to see the pupil as it contracts. The iris is actually only a small part of the white eyeball, most of which cannot be seen because it is under the eyelids. Look at the upper and lower eyelids. Notice that they cover part of the iris even when they are open. The opening between the two lids is usually a variation on an almond or football shape. If you look closely at the juncture of the two lids, you can see the tear ducts. The eyelids protect the eye and allow us to sleep. Notice that there are eyelashes at the ends of both upper and lower lids. They keep dust and dirt from getting into our eyes. Many artists paint a very tiny

gleam or white dot on the side of the iris. Look again at the eye and try to see a small white reflection on the iris. In many paintings, a white dot makes it appear that the eye is three-dimensional and gives the illusion that the eye is sparkling.

Take a few minutes to review the parts of the eyes. Be sure to advise children to draw the eyes simultaneously; it is difficult to get eyes to look right when painting one eye at a time. Students should build eyes by drawing both outside shapes, then both irises, and so on. The following is an easy way to teach children to draw or paint eyes. It can serve as a beginning point from which children will naturally create their own variations.

Painting Eyes

MATERIALS: Paints in white and black plus a few eye colors, white chalk, small brushes, strips of manila paper or newsprint practice paper, water dishes.

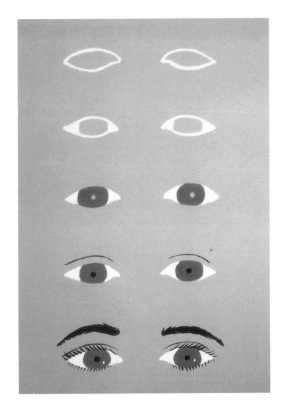

It is helpful to give students a step-by-step approach to painting eyes: Look closely at the overall shape of the opening between the upper and lower eyelids; you will see an almond or oval shape. Using white paint and a small brush, paint two eye shapes. Leave a space the width of an eye between the two shapes. Then paint the whites of the eyes. Use an eye color to paint the irises. Using black paint and a small brush, paint the pupils and a line for the upper and lower eyelids. Add eyelashes and eyebrows. Add a tiny white dot in each eye as a highlight. Be sure the highlight is in the same position on each eye.

Children seem to feel quite accomplished when they are able to approximate what eyes look like. After painting eyes, it is natural to want to try to paint faces. Take a few moments to have children feel the ins and outs of their heads and faces. Make a distinction between the top of the head and where the hairline actually begins. Ask children to feel where their noses begin at the ridge of the eyebrows, and ask them to feel their upper and lower lips. Instruct children to feel their jawbones and the shapes of their ears.

While working, it is easy for children to get so caught up in getting the details right that they fail to look at, or think about, the overall shape of the head and general placement of features. It is, therefore, helpful to point out the basic proportions of the head and face before sending children off to work. At the elementary level, the main emphasis is on looking closely, not on achieving exact pro-portions. But it is also important to teach children — especially those at the upper elementary level — some of the discoveries about proportions that have proven to be helpful to artists. Be aware that many children are inclined to do expressive work in which proportions are distorted. This says something about how they are thinking and feeling, which, after all, is an important purpose of creating art. So give children a few guidelines to think about, then enjoy and delight in the variations that appear.

Children are often amazed by the likenesses they can capture when simply directed to paint the person sitting across from them using black paint and a brush. Having a few pieces of newsprint on which to practice helps children feel more comfortable. It is not necessary to have painted eyes before doing brush paintings of heads and shoulders, but it can be helpful.

Rather than presenting a formula for diagramming heads, indicate some general guidelines. Use your hands to show the top and bottom of the head. Sometimes children think the hairline is the top of the head. Help them see that the hairline actually begins farther down. Point out that eyes generally fall halfway between the top and bottom of the head. The nose generally lies halfway between the eye and chin, and the mouth rests halfway between the bottom of the nose and the chin. Ears lie parallel to the tops of the eyes and extend to the bottom of the nose.

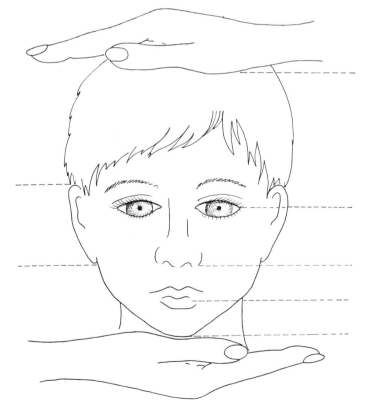

When focusing on facial features and expression, a few lines or strokes can often be very descriptive. Georges Rouault, *Nurse*, 1913. Black crayon and watercolor, 11½″ x 8″ (30 cm x 20 cm). Smith College Museum of Art, Northampton, Massachusetts.

Brush Drawings of Heads and Shoulders

MATERIALS: Black paint, medium brushes, white paper.

Look closely at the shape of your model's jaw, then paint a variation of a U shape. Add the neck and shoulders.

Paint the eyes, nose, mouth, eyebrows and ears. Paint the hair using a texture stroke. Then paint patterns, textures and clothing details. *Portrait of Alex*, David Barowsky, grade 5.

Encourage students to look at other classmates and add them to their pictures. Add other points of view. Lindsay Fogg-Willets, grade 3.

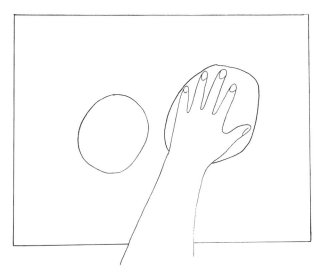

Use your finger to plan the placement of the two heads. Make the adult's head as big as your hand. A child's head would be a little smaller. Then draw the main head shapes onto your paper with oil pastels.

Use oil pastels to draw the rest of the bodies. Draw the features of the faces and add line and texture details for the hair, clothing and background. Don't color in the larger areas.

Planning a Composition from Memory

When working from a theme, such as "Me and A Special Adult," rather than from direct observation, the motivation part of the lesson is very important. Encourage children to share experiences they have had with the people they are going to portray in their pictures. What do they especially enjoy doing together — playing a game, reading or cooking? Actually trying out the pose to be painted is also extremely helpful. Ask children to be aware of the head positions as well as the positions of arms and hands.

Paintings of more than one person or of a person with a prop such as a stuffed animal, hat or piece of sports equipment is actually easier and less threatening than a painting of one person in a straightforward position. This is because the emphasis changes from focusing on features and proportions to focusing on composition.

Working from memory or imagination takes more thinking and planning than working from direct observation. "Sketching" with a finger or dry brush before actually placing marks on the paper saves a lot of frustration and a lot of starting over. Teach children to use their hand size when planning the size and placement of the head of each subject. Remember that a child's head is smaller than that of an adult. It is helpful to begin by placing the head shapes on the paper. Adding the neck, shoulders and arms follows easily from these. Focus children by asking them to tell you the themes of their pictures and to indicate the positions of the subjects before they begin.

Children may use oil pastels on white paper to draw the structure of their compositions. Encourage them to add background details as well as details and textures on the people and their clothing. Tell them not to color in because they will be using paint to add areas of color. When drawings are complete, tempera blocks or watercolors may be used to add color to the compositions. When children are finished, have them each write a sentence about their pictures.

Use watercolor or tempera blocks to fill in large areas. Paint directly over the oil pastels. *Grandma is Reading Me a Book,* Britt Harlow, grade 1.

Me and My Dad Playing Checkers, Ben Dion, grade 1.

Gallery of People Paintings

During their art periods, children in the fourth grade at the Smith College Campus School spend the year studying the arts of Native Americans. In preparation for painting people, children looked at examples of paintings by several Native American artists. Rather than concentrating on features of the face, children concentrated on the designs and colors that are woven into fabrics and blankets by many Native American tribes. Jani Christiansen, grade 4.

To complete these life-size figures of people dressed in winter clothing, children began with the head and facial features on a piece of oak tag. During the next class, the upper and lower bodies were painted. The emphasis was on creating textures and patterns to brighten up winter clothing. At the end, each body section was cut out and stapled together. *Winter People*, first-graders, Jackson Street School. Art teacher: Jacklyn Coe.

Children studying Colonial America looked at early American portrait paintings done by limners, who traveled across the country painting portraits. The children painted their own portraits trying to recapture the style of those paintings. Colonial portrait, Alice Kidder, grade 5.

Summary

PAINTING PEOPLE: Painting figures builds on the approaches used in painting animals. Children should be encouraged to try more than one way of painting the form of a person. They should also practice brush drawings of the human form from several points of view.

Working from models simulates the artist's studio and is usually a new and exciting experience for children. They can experience the skills necessary to posing, and they can also experience the challenge of conveying the position of the model with paint on a two-dimensional surface. You can help children appreciate the difficulty of this task and the reason for practice. It is especially important to show the works of many different artists who paint people and to point out what is working well in each student's brush sketches. Position, expression, freedom of the brushstroke, size of the figure, attention to the outline, expressive details and approach are all aspects of capturing the feeling of a figure with paint.

Strategies for mixing skin tones and painting in brush sketches are also important to explore at this point.

HEADS AND FACES: To paint a face or portrait, children are asked to analyze the shapes, placement and proportion of each facial feature. By focusing only on eyes, children experience painting one feature in detail and isolation. Once they are able to paint a facsimile of an eye, they can add the other facial features to compose a face.

Once children have successfully painted one head, they can make subtle changes to features to create a variety of different characters. They can also practice creating likenesses of one another.

PAINTING FROM MEMORY: When painting from memory, your motivation and your students' planning and thinking ahead of time are extremely important. Using fingers to "sketch" the compositions and hands to get a sense of the size of each head helps children step back and get an overall feeling for the compositions they are about to create. Being able to think ahead and plan is a skill necessary in art and in all of life. Give children a chance to try this skill by refraining from handing out oil pastels or crayons for a few minutes.

An excellent mixed media combination is achieved by using a drawing medium such as crayons or oil pastels to plan and adding paint to the drawn structure.

Part Three

Alternative Approaches and Aesthetics

The strokes and techniques used with black ink painting and watercolor are specific and precise. Sometimes it is helpful to work freely and expressively for a while before teaching strokes and painting procedures. Children can combine previous discoveries with newfound skills. Supplies and skills used in both black ink painting and watercolor can also be used to do any of the activities in earlier chapters.

Indelible marker and watercolor. Kate Marantz, age 5.

The idea for this lesson came from a scroll painting that showed grasses silhouetted against a large, yellow-orange harvest moon. Children were each given a yellow square of construction paper from which they cut a moon and pasted it to a long, gray rectangle of construction paper. Students were directed to silhouette some grasses against the moon and make some grasses thick and thin, dark and light, short and tall, vertical or diagonal. Top: Cyrena Koury, grade 2. Bottom: Chip O'Dowd, grade 2.

11 Black Ink Painting of East Asia

Exposing children to a few East Asian brush techniques and a bit of the philosophy behind those techniques helps children appreciate a very different painting tradition. Discipline, practice and a ritualized learning sequence characterize the black ink painting traditions of China, Japan and Korea. Emphasis is placed on preparing oneself for the act of painting. The idea of contemplating and trying to convey the essential life force or spirit of the subject is also important. For children raised in a Western culture, trying black ink painting brings up new ways to think about the purpose of creating art.

Brush ink painting is an ancient art and basic painting tradition that began in China as early as the fourth century BC and later spread to Japan and Korea. It is the major form of painting in East Asia. As in Western painting, there are many diverse styles and schools of brush ink painting. Broadly speaking, there are two major styles. In one the artist takes care to show each tiny detail — each feather on a bird or part of a flower. The second major style is more expressionistic. In this style, the artist is

more interested in expressing an idea. The aim is to "say" as much as possible with the fewest brushstrokes. Paintings done in this style are completed in one sitting so the sense of harmony painters feel with their subjects is not interrupted.

In East Asia, the whole idea about just what the brushstroke is supposed to be and do is quite different from Western notions of the brush and its capabilities. There is, in a sense, a respect for the power of the brush and the act of painting. *The Mustard Seed Garden Manual of Painting,* written in 1679–1701, which describes the "tao," or way, of Chinese painting, illustrates thirty different ways to use a brush to paint dotted leaves. The descriptions are vivid and include "dotting like a sprinkling of pepper," "dotting like pine needles," "dotting like mouse tracks," "dotting in three strokes coming together," "dotting like blades of drooping grass" and "dotting in blobs, like a whirlpool." There does not seem to be anything in the painterly traditions of the West documenting so many specific ways to represent one thing. Brushstrokes used in black ink painting

Black ink painting strokes are similar to those used in calligraphy. Traditionally in the East, calligraphy was produced with a brush rather than a pen, as it was in the West. The three sets of characters mean "black ink painting" or "black ink picture." They are written, from right to left, in Chinese, Korean and Japanese. By Yoon Park, 1990.

actually cause children to use finger and arm muscles they might not otherwise use for painting. They present children with new options for gaining control over the brush.

While overpainting is common in the West, it is uncommon in the traditions of East Asian painting, where each brushstroke is visible. A painter is encouraged to visualize each stroke — where it will begin, how it will lie on the paper and how it will end. Understatement and simplicity are also highly valued. The white space of the paper is as important as the brushstrokes that give the painting form. Space in the Eastern tradition is viewed as very wide and deep. The edges of a paper block out one tiny part of the vast space of the universe. Space continues beyond the edges of the paper, just as thoughts and ideas continue.

The basic materials of ink painting are black ink, a bamboo brush, clear water and white paper. The colors of ink painting are black and the many subtle tones of gray that lie between black and the pure white of the paper. The brushstroke itself creates subtle tones as each stroke gives form to the white surface of the paper. Traditional Japanese sumi(ink)–e(painting) is painted only with black, while traditional and modern Chinese paintings use color.

Before working with the brush, it is the custom to clear one's mind of all distractions. In some traditions, a simple meditation, or centering exercise, is used to ready oneself for painting. A painter then concentrates on a segment of nature. Plants, branches, blossoms, mountains, landscapes, birds, animals and people are all traditional subjects for study. It is believed that, through the act of brush ink painting, a person might see him or herself in perspective, as just one small part of a greater universe. According to Confucian philosophy, one should work at cultivating oneself to become a better, more moral person. Ink painting is part of this process. In executing each brushstroke, one's entire mind and body should be focused. Painting, in a sense, can be a vehicle for clearing the mind of destructive thoughts. It is a way to place oneself in harmony with nature, with the smallest to the largest living things. Traditionally, painting was important training for gentleman scholars, that is, men of culture. Anyone considered educated or cultured studied ink painting along with history, science, mathematics and philosophy and, in some cases, the martial arts. It is said that "Those who are skilled in painting will live long because life created through the sweep of the brush can strengthen life itself."

In order to take the activities suggested here further and learn more about this tradition of painting, consult one of the many fine books on ink painting listed in the Bibliography.

Materials

Children enjoy touching and using ink painting supplies. They are intrigued by the act of grinding ink sticks on grinding stones and trying bamboo brushes. These materials can be used again and again, so they are definitely worth collecting when possible. However, the ink painting techniques illustrated here can be learned with watercolor brushes and watercolors or black tempera cakes. Even watered down black tempera paint will work. When using watercolors, a single pan of black pigment works best at first, so that children will not be tempted by all the colors.

Like Western brushes, there are many varieties of bamboo brushes. Get good quality, medium-size, basic, resilient stroke brushes. One basic brush can be used many ways. Details and very thin lines can be painted with the tiny point of the brush. Wider lines can be painted by varying the pressure placed on the bristles of the brush. Very thick lines and areas can be painted with the side of the brush. By putting less ink on the brush, the hairs tend to split and the painter can create a dry-brush effect.

A bamboo brush is constructed differently from a Western one. It has a kind of well that holds a good amount of ink within its bristles. Because of this quality, ink painters can execute many brushstrokes and sometimes even complete paintings without stopping to re-ink their brushes and break concentration.

New bamboo brushes come sized with protective plastic tops. Before using a brush, remove the sizing by swishing the brush in cool or lukewarm water for a few moments. Don't replace the plastic caps when you are done because they can inadvertently break the bristles. To care for a brush once it has been used, swish it in water, wipe it on a paper towel, then stroke the brush over a bar of soap so it forms a point. Leave the soap in the brush and let it dry flat; this stiffens the bristles.

The materials of black ink painting include an ink stick, grinding stone, bamboo brush, clear water and white paper.

To use the grinding stone, place a small amount of water into the well, or "sea." Moisten the ink stick by dipping it into the well. Then grind the ink stick against the "land." Repeat this sequence until the ink is dark; this takes some time. The blackest ink is taken from the "land." Lighter tones are obtained by dipping into the "sea" and into clear water.

Dried ink sticks are made from a combination of soot and animal glue. They are often decorated with gold designs. Ink can also be purchased in liquid form. Like ink sticks, grinding stones come in many shapes and sizes. Basically, grinding stones are flat with an indentation or well at one end. The Japanese refer to the well as the "sea" and the raised portion of the grinding stone as the "land."

Ink paintings were traditionally painted on silk or on any of a variety of delicate papers. Paper for ink painting comes in rolls, tablets and sheets and is usually listed under the heading "rice paper." This is misleading, since few papers are actually made from rice by-products. Papers vary greatly, and many are quite beautiful. In some cases, flowers and fibers are part of the paper. Papers for ink painting are sized with a mixture of alum and glue. Each paper has one smooth side and one rough side. Paint is usually applied to the smooth side. A paper is chosen for its ability to accept ink while allowing for a wide range of gray tones. This absorbency is one reason brush paintings must be done quickly. Painting on a small piece of rice paper is an interesting and new experience for children. They will probably find it difficult to paint on traditional rice paper.

Though it is not white, newsprint absorbs ink easily — but not nearly as quickly as rice paper. Newsprint can be used for all of the exercises in this chapter. It works well for children to experiment on newsprint before working on rice paper or standard white paper. Dippity Dye paper has proven to be a reasonable compromise. It is whiter than newsprint and looks like rice paper, yet it is not quite as absorbent. Rolls of paper used to cover examining tables in doctors' offices work well too. Get the mat, not shiny, paper.

Brush Ink Painting in the Classroom

Try playing Japanese bamboo flute music or other classical music that is quieting and soothing as children put on their smocks or enter the room. The gentle sounds evoke a contemplative mood. They let children know that they are about to experience something new. Using music as an introduction is a powerful teaching tool, but it is not a necessary one. This experience also works well without music.

Use a map or globe to locate East Asia. Explain that children in China, Japan and Korea begin their calligraphy and ink painting lessons by preparing their minds and bodies for the task ahead. You can encourage children to try this by asking them to pay attention to the way they are sitting and to sit up straight. Demonstrate that proper posture is necessary to allow the arm to swing freely.

As a second focus, ask children to become conscious of their breathing. In the West, we don't typically pay much attention to how we use our breath. But East Asians have found that one's breath can be an inner source of energy. Ask children to breathe deeply — to bring their breath all the way down to their abdomens so it fills their chests. They can then slowly exhale, allowing all air to be expelled. Closing eyes is helpful. Children can picture the air filling up their bellies and chests, then gradually leaving. Through this short, meditative exercise, children can concentrate on their breath and its pathway through the body rather than on other distractions. They can clear their minds and prepare themselves for the discipline of painting.

Speak softly as you dip your ink stick into the well, or "sea," of the grinding stone to pick up some water. Rub the moistened ink on the raised portion, or "land." As you repeat this procedure, tell children that preparing the ink is also a way to loosen up the arm and ready oneself for painting. It is the preparation of the person and materials that takes time in brush ink painting. The actual painting is done quickly.

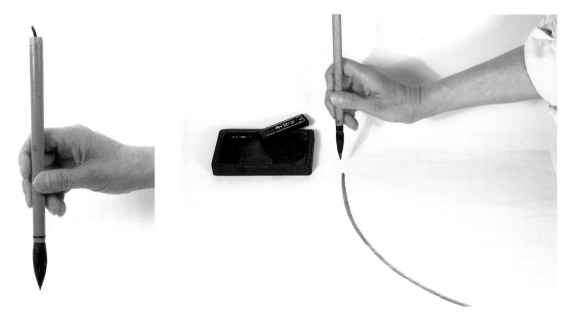

Hold the bamboo brush slightly above the center of the handle between the thumb and first two fingers. Let the handle rest against the remaining two fingers. Keep the brush upright for strength.

The hand and arm move together as one unit from the shoulder or elbow. The wrist remains stationary.

Demonstrate how to hold a bamboo brush. Pass out brushes so that each student can get the feel of one. Tell students to keep their wrists stationary but their arms easy. Students may go through the various strokes with you in the air before trying them out with ink. Try moving the brush in a circle. Try strokes that go from left to right and from bottom to top. Think of the brushstroke as beginning somewhere off the page, briefly touching the page, and then continuing beyond the page.

Each brushstroke or group of brushstrokes flows from the painter's exhalation or spirit — from that which is in the painter's heart — leaving a record of its movement on paper. Brushstrokes are sometimes referred to as the "heart-prints" of the painter. Practice inhaling before a brushstroke and exhaling as you paint. Let each brushstroke flow from an inner impulse deep within the center of your being.

The oblique position is an alternate way to hold the brush. It is generally used to create thick brushstrokes. Lay the bristles down flat, straighten the brush, and push up with your arm.

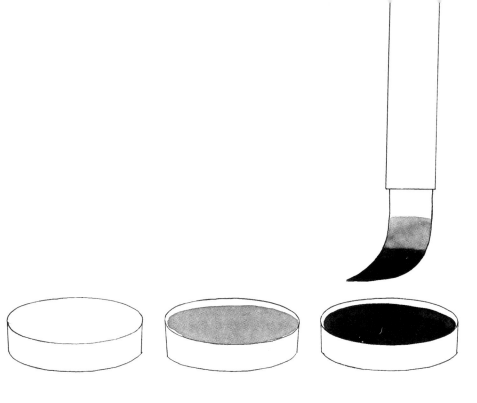

To create a light-to-dark gradation of ink, try the "three ink method." Dip the whole brush in clear water first. Then dip it halfway in dark gray ink. Finally, dip the tip into pure black. When used on its side, the brush should produce three gradations.

Even though a watercolor brush is not constructed in the same way as a bamboo brush, it can be used to try most ink painting brushstrokes. Sometimes bamboo brushes sold in lots to schools are not the best quality and do not form good points. In this case, good watercolor brushes work better.

Experimenting with a Bamboo Brush

MATERIALS: Ink sticks, grinding stones, bamboo brushes, white paper.

As children work, circulate through the room helping them experience the correct posture, brush position and use of the arm. Then, let them try the strokes in their own ways. The goal is not to paint as a master of ink painting would do, but simply to experience a new approach to painting. Once children have tried all the strokes, give them new pieces of paper. They can use all the strokes to make a design or painting of their own choice. Often the brushstrokes themselves will suggest ideas for paintings.

The "three ink method" can give a thick line a three-dimensional quality.

Instruct students to experiment with basic brush strokes: To begin exploring the bamboo brush and what it can do, start by making dabs. Fully charge the brush with ink, but don't make it so wet that it drips. Stroke the brush on an absorbent paper towel to remove excess ink if the brush is too wet, or to form a point. Then press the brush to the paper and lift it straight up. Try this several times. Try making a palm leaf, daisy, orchid, and lotus blossom out of dabs. How are the dab strokes in the daisy and the orchid placed differently?

Try the bamboo leaf strokes, bone strokes, eyebrow stroke, swirl, and grasses. Be sure the tip of the brush forms a point. Sit up straight, and breathe deeply a few times. Keep your wrist stiff, but let your arm move easily from your shoulder or elbow. The hand and forearm should not touch the paper. Practice each stroke until you can do it well. Be sure to pay attention to where the stroke begins and ends. Try to make some strokes very black and others in lighter tones of gray.

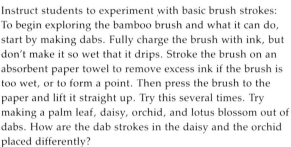

On the left, the artist shows the strokes for painting a flying duck in step-by-step order. A suggestion of foreground grasses, middle ground cattails and silhouettes of ducks flying south in the distance creates a feeling of deep space with only a few lines. *Flying South*, Belinda Zucker, 1990. Courtesy of the artist.

Painting a Bamboo Grove

Bamboo paintings seem to embody the essential spirit of East Asia. Bamboo grows throughout all four seasons. It is a perfect example of strength combined with grace, strong yet yielding. In Japan, sumi–e students start painting by practicing with bamboo as the subject. Sometimes they continue painting bamboo for many years. To paint bamboo with subtle skill is probably not possible for the beginner. However, children can enjoy experimenting with a few of the strokes they have practiced and create surprisingly pleasing paintings fairly quickly. Painting bamboo is an exercise in composition and in using different gradations of black.

Hold your brush in the oblique position. Sit up straight. Inhale deeply, then exhale. Pause and press down on your brush at the beginning and end of each stroke. Sometimes it helps to use your little finger to steady and guide your arm.

Paint bamboo stems from the bottom of the page to the top, in the direction in which they grow. Make some bamboo stems vertical and some diagonal. Make some thin and others thick. Make some light and others dark. Make some close together and some farther apart. Stems can continue beyond the page.

Using the tip of your brush, add the small horizontal joints of each stem.

Paint the bamboo leaves using the leaf stroke.

Join the leaves to the stems with thin branching strokes. The small red mark at the bottom left was made by the artist's chop or stamp. Bamboo painting, Dora Chen, 1990. Courtesy of the artist.

Sarah Rundquist, grade 4.

Daniel Pfieffer-Kotz, grade 2.

Masterwork and child's copy. Carina Wohl, grade 3.

Another way to try a variety of brushstrokes is to copy from brush ink masters. This works well if you can collect a variety of brush ink paintings from calendars or magazines. Though copying is not something we usually encourage, it is a major part of any brush painter's training in East Asia. By copying a master's painting, the apprentice experiences the master's brush techniques, sense of composition and use of space as well as his or her inspiration and vision. Until recently, paintings were not sold commercially in East Asia the way they are here in the West. Art was closely integrated with life. Being copied was considered a great compliment. As they copy a master's painting, encourage children to try to duplicate the master's lines, the tones of gray and black, and the way lines are spaced on the page.

Choosing Subjects

It is especially effective to use ink painting strokes to paint from direct observation. This involves analyzing the subject for lines and shapes that can be depicted with different brushstrokes. In choosing subjects for brush ink painting, think in terms of line. Does the subject have a variety of contrasting linear forms? Is it simple enough that children can pick out one "line" at a time? Are there both thick and thin lines? Dried grasses, flowers and weeds make excellent subjects for painting in fall. In winter, branches cut from different varieties of deciduous and coniferous trees work well. In spring, flowering branches such as forsythia, dogwood, crabapple and pussy willow have proven to be successful subjects. Varieties of cacti have distinct shapes and lines that children enjoy trying to capture with paint. Have a few different subjects available so children can switch subjects when they are done with their first paintings.

Painting Birds

Once children begin to feel comfortable using the brush, they can try to paint birds. A collection of bird postcards or pictures is fairly easy to accumulate and enables children to study the details and position of their subjects. Of course, actual stuffed or live birds would be preferable for study if available. Children are always surprised by how well they can capture the spirit of the bird using brush ink techniques. Ask children to try painting one of the birds in a step-by-step fashion using linear, oblique and dark and light strokes. Children can then work directly from bird photos. Practicing the individual strokes that will be used to paint the bird is also a helpful way to warm up for painting.

MATERIALS: Pictures that clearly show the shape, textures and markings of specific birds work best. *Ranger Rick, World, National Geographic Magazine,* and *Smithsonian* magazines are all excellent sources of pictures. Painting supplies remain the same as for previous activities.

Dried grasses are easy to find in the fall. When arranging them, choose a few very different kinds of grasses and place them far enough apart so children can see the individual lines. A lump of oil-based, non-drying modeling clay makes a handy base.

This mural of flower and grass silhouettes was painted in a corner of the room. As children completed their individual paintings, they added the flowers and grasses they had practiced to the mural.

Direct students to try painting a parrot: Paint the crest with bamboo leaf strokes. Paint the eye and beak using the very tip of the pointed brush. Paint the body, the wings and the tail using lines. Use an oblique stroke for the branch. Add the legs and feet with small dark dots and lines. Use at least one value of gray, and then use black for contrast.

Direct students to try painting a sparrow: Start with the beak and eye. Use lines and areas of gray for the body. Use dots and dabs for the feathers and the feet.

After painting several birds using only black ink or paint, it is exciting to use watercolors. Students will find they have a vocabulary of brushstrokes to use with this new medium. Lydia Guaio, *Woodpecker*. Collection of Dr. and Mrs. Philip A. Weisman.

The basic ways of using a brush and preparing oneself to paint can be used effectively with many of the other painting activities in this book. It is especially fun to use these approaches when working with watercolors.

Summary

Correct posture, deep breathing, precise ways of holding and moving a brush, and specific strokes are emphasized when readying oneself for the almost spiritual act of brush ink painting. The placement, darkness or lightness and character of each brushstroke defines the white space of the paper.

Help children experience and appreciate this ancient and dramatically different painting tradition as a way of fostering cross-cultural understanding. Compare and contrast a traditional brush ink painting with a Western painting. Ask children to point out differences and similarities.

"I loved to collect lightning bugs when I was a child. One night I kept them in a jar by my bed when I went to sleep. I dreamed that the bugs escaped from the jar, and that a whole variety of insects was trying to bite me. I woke up screaming and let the fireflies go free." Adding watercolor to detailed sketches done with indelible markers, or even with regular fineline markers, is an effective way to dramatize drawings. Cathy Weisman Topal, *Nightmare,* 1970. Pen and ink and watercolor.

12 Watercolors

Like black ink, watercolors flow more freely than tempera paints and require more control. Like black ink painting, painting with watercolors is a quick way of working. In both painting mediums, the approach is carefully thought through beforehand, but the actual painting is done deliberately and quickly. One of the differences between the two media is that the number of color choices complicates the watercolor painting process. Rather than concentrating on the brushstrokes, the value of gray, the amount of water to be used and the placement of subject on paper, children get diverted easily by color choices, options for mixing colors, the need to rinse and wipe brushes between colors and the need to replenish muddy water supplies. For all these reasons, it makes sense to practice black ink painting techniques before introducing watercolors. Then, when children do begin to work with watercolors, they will already have a certain amount of skill.

Nina Frank, grade 3.

Concentrating on Brushstrokes

One basic watercolor technique emphasizes brush-strokes; all the black ink painting strokes can be applied to this method of using watercolors. In fact, after experimenting with ink painting, children will be much more able to control watercolors. Children will enjoy painting watercolor flowers by concentrating on individual lines and shapes as they did when painting bamboo and grasses with black ink.

Painting Watercolor Flowers

Studying one flower with its leaves and stem in detail helps a child learn how to approach painting any flower. When choosing flowers for children to paint, think in terms of dots, dabs, lines and shapes. Make them simple so children can paint them easily. Practice the individual brushstrokes that are necessary to paint each part of the flower.

Combine individual brushstrokes to paint a flower or branch.

Now try painting a flower in color.

Children looked closely at one branch or flower and painted it. Then they switched flowers with their neighbors and added another flower to their gardens. Meredith Reeves, kindergarten.

Fuschia, Thalia Brown,
grade 5.

When introducing watercolors, demonstrate that the amount of water and pigment changes the value of the color. Encourage children to use both light and dark values in their paintings. Leaving a white space between areas of color keeps them from running together. Illustration by Susan Dennen.

Watercolor materials consist of a set of watercolor paints, water dish, paper towel and a watercolor brush. Teach children to place a drop of water into each pan of color before they start to work. This softens the color pigments and helps generate more vibrant color. Claire Topal, grade 6.

The colors that are generated by watercolor paints are transparent. Unlike in tempera paintings, the colors in watercolor paintings remain clear, glowing and vibrant even when paintings have dried. Watercolors are handy to transport and use in a classroom. They work well when added to drawings, since lines show through the paint. In fact, before being considered a legitimate painting medium in its own right, watercolors were used to add tints to sketches, engravings and etchings. Oil was thought to be the acceptable medium for the final painting. It was only in 1804 that the Society of Watercolour Painters was founded in England and shortly after that, that watercolor became a popular and acceptable painting medium. Taking the time to give children a chance to practice controlling watercolors is well worth the effort, since there are so many ways watercolors can be used in the elementary classroom.

Watercolor paints for the elementary classroom generally come in kits of eight basic colors with a medium-size watercolor brush. When preparing to use watercolors with a group of children, you need a set of watercolors and a water container for each two children. The larger the water container, the fewer times it will need to be emptied and refilled. Fill containers only half or three-quarters full to avoid spills.

The basic, round number 6 or 7 camel hair brush is sufficient for most watercolor projects. However, number 10 or 12 watercolor brushes for laying washes, for oil pastel resist projects and for large group murals are also handy. Children enjoy using number 1, 2 or 3 brushes for painting tiny details. It is worthwhile to invest in good quality brushes and take care of them. Any of these brushes can also be used with tempera paint.

Watercolor is most effective on a good student-grade absorbent white paper or special watercolor paper. Order a package of watercolor paper, or buy a pad. Papers can be cut to postcard size (3″ x 5″ or 4″ x 6″) for most watercolor experiments. Larger 5″ x 7″ and 8″ x 10″ papers can be used for final paintings. Watercolor paper is heavier and has "tooth," which means that it is slightly textured and holds or grips the paint in unique ways. When water is applied, paper has the tendency to warp or curl. In general, thick paper warps less than thin paper. To prevent curling, it is helpful to have children tape their papers at the four corners to boards or pieces of cardboard. Theoretically, papers should be left taped to boards until they are dry. However, if papers are removed when they are almost dry, you can allow the paintings to dry completely, then make a pile of the dry paintings and leave them under a few heavy books overnight to flatten again. Paintings can also be done without taping papers to boards; papers can simply be flattened once they have dried, if that is necessary.

One of the most difficult aspects of teaching children to use watercolors is teaching them to thoroughly rinse their brushes and wipe them dry to see whether they are, indeed, clean. An absorbent paper towel, sponge or cloth is important for this reason. The other difficult concept for children to control is how much water to use.

Paint should flow easily from the brush. When the paint does not flow, it is a signal to get more paint and water.

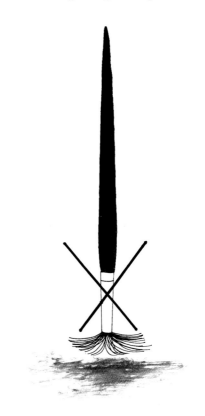

You should not have to scrub.

Painting on wet paper — serendipitous painting — is a nonthreatening, exciting way to become familiar with the characteristics of watercolor and to practice controlling the amount of water on paper. *Serendipity* is the appearance of an unexpected but valuable or agreeable thing. Children enjoy watching colored areas magically spread themselves out on moistened paper. They can see firsthand that water is really the magic element in watercolor painting. They can share discoveries with one another to learn how to create a variety of effects. Have children try more than one experiment on wet paper. The first painting can be just tiny dots, the second can be an experiment with dabs, the third can be an experiment with lines. Serendipitous paintings make colorful backgrounds for silhouette pictures, line drawings and prints. These watercolor experiments can also be used as postcards or stationery.

While working, encourage children to get a sense of how much pigment they need to use to make intense colors as opposed to pale tints. Point out that, in watercolor painting, the white of the paper shows through the paint to create a tint. If a clear white is desired, the paper itself is left without pigment. In order to remove excess water, demonstrate how to "erase," which is a technique to control the amount of water on paper. Children like knowing this technique and find it intriguing as well as useful.

Serendipitous Paintings

MATERIALS: White paper — try several small pieces of different size rectangles as well as one larger (8" x 11") paper, watercolors, basic number 6 or 7 watercolor brushes and large wash brushes if desired, sponges, paper towels.

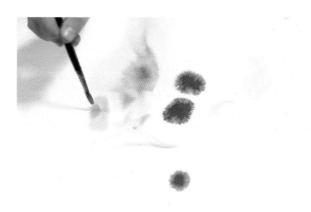

Students can achieve interesting effects by using watercolor on wet paper: Use a wash brush, a sponge or your fingertips to wet your paper. It should look shiny when looked at from the side. Then tickle one color with the brush, working water into the pigment so that the color will be bright. (The word "tickle" helps children realize how little pressure is necessary.) Use the tip of the brush to paint dots all over the paper. This exercise helps children develop control over the brush while they are concentrating on placement.

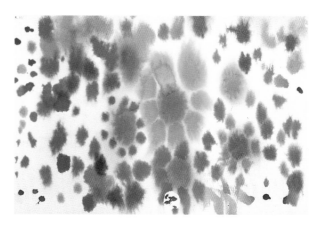

Try many colors. Watch them spread. LivAnna Homstead, age 4.

When your paper has dried, turn it around and look at it from different points of view. What forms can you find? Use your imagination. Use a fineline black marker to bring these forms to life. Margaret Rayno-Quirk, grade 2.

Wet a second paper. This time see what happens when you paint lines. Experiment with lines from the line chart, Chapter 1.

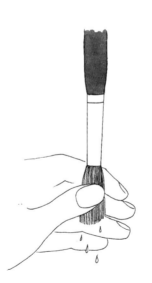

When there is too much water in one part of the painting, try erasing. Wash your brush well to remove all color pigments. Squeeze the bristles with your hand or wipe the brush on a paper towel to remove the water.

Now touch your dry brush to the puddle. Watch it soak up the excess water. Repeat this step if necessary.

Laying a Wash

Once children have had some experience with emphasizing brushstrokes using watercolors, teach them how to lay a wash. Washes characterize watercolor paintings, and laying a wash is the other basic watercolor technique upon which children can expand in their own unique ways. In many watercolor paintings, wash and stroke techniques are combined. The word *wash* implies water, which is the most important ingredient in watercolor painting, especially in laying down a wash. It is important to use more water than paint. Washes create an atmospheric feeling or background that can be painted over.

It is easy to expand on the basic wash technique to create multicolored washes. These washes can seem almost mystical. Use them to create atmospheric effects. They can evoke sky and land formations and suggest different times of day. To create a wash that goes from dark to light, or a "graded wash," instead of continuing with the pre-mixed wash color, use clear water to bring the puddle down to the bottom of the paper. Making the puddle turn into controlled drips creates still other unusual results. The mixture of technique, control and serendipity makes this lesson especially fun for any age-group.

Experimenting with Washes

MATERIALS: Small and large white papers — two or three for each child, tape, boards, number 10 or 12 watercolor brushes, pans of watercolors, paper towels.

Direct students to lay a wash: Tape your paper to a board at the corners. Moisten your colors. On the lid, mix a wash color and add lots of water to it. Load your brush full of this mixture. Beginning at the top corner of the paper, move the brush all the way across to the other side. You should complete this with one stroke. Watch a puddle form at the bottom of the painted area.

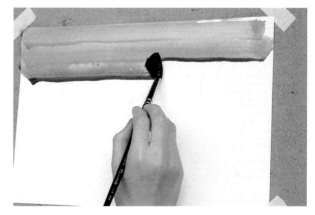

Load the brush again with the wash color. Starting at the edge of the paper, pick up the puddle and sweep the brush all the way to the other side of the paper. The puddle should form again at the bottom of the painted area. Repeat this procedure until you have completed your wash. It is important to work fairly quickly so the puddle does not dry out. If you don't get a puddle, either you are not slanting your board enough or you are not using enough water.

Multicolor Washes

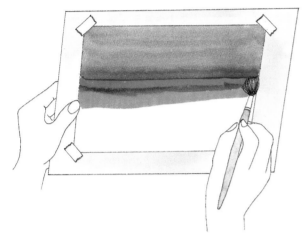

Mix a wash color and paint it from one side of your paper to the other. Allow a puddle to form. Continue this color as many times as you like. Wash your brush and load it with a new wash color. Use this color to pick up the puddle and continue the wash.

Make some stripes very narrow and others very broad. Try leaving some small white spaces between the bands of color. Repeat at least one color for unity. To create still other unusual effects, try turning the paper while you work so drips form. Continue the wash to the end of the paper.

In fall and winter, the branching patterns of trees show up clearly against a sunset sky. Draw trees with a black crayon, and discuss the way the branches intertwine. Then use the wash techniques to paint a sky. The waxy crayon will resist the watercolor paint. Black crayon tree silhouettes with wash, Aaron Chandler-Worth, grade 6.

Painting outside is sure to be a special experience for children. Every child can be successful with this lesson.

Painter at Paradise Pond, Sage Wasson, grade 5.

Painting Outside

One reason watercolors are such a popular painting medium is that they are much easier than oil paints to transport and use outdoors. Painting outside is a wonderful way for children to experience and study their environment. However, firm behavioral guidelines should be set beforehand. It is also important to explain directions for the art lesson and procedures for getting and keeping track of supplies before venturing outdoors. That way, children can begin working as soon as they have found places to sit. Be sure to scout out your destination and possible sitting places before you actually bring a class! Laying out sections of newspaper to serve as seating pads is a good way to designate seating places when it is not windy. You don't have to venture far. Paintings of the school building and grounds are always fun to try. When it is not feasible to go outdoors, working from postcards or pictures of landscapes and city views is one way to pick out the horizon line and other main lines in a setting.

Making a beginning sketch is an important first step to painting a scene. A sketch sets up the basic composition and delineates a few of the main objects and textures in the scene. Just a few lines set down beforehand make painting in specific areas much easier. Children can choose to do a panoramic view or a small close-up.

It is also important to help children become aware that, when using watercolors, they have to paint the light areas before painting the dark areas. Also, remind children to leave the white of the paper when they want the color white to be in a specific place in their paintings. Have a box of facial tissues handy for children to mop up excess paint.

Painting from Direct Observation

MATERIALS: White 11" x 16" paper taped to boards, black indelible markers or black crayons, watercolors, wash brushes and small brushes, water, newspapers, paper towels or facial tissues.

With a little guidance, students can be quite successful painting outdoor scenes: Spend a few minutes looking at your scene and sketching it out with a finger to get a sense of placement and size relationships. Then draw the main "strong" or important lines and shapes of objects you see. Add a few lines to indicate texture.

Paint large washes of color in the main areas of your composition. Begin with lighter colors. You may wish to wet an area of your paper, such as the sky, before adding colors.

Add darker colors to your painting while the paper is still damp. Repeat colors for unity. Mix several variations of a color — such as blue, blue-green and lavender blue. Use a small brush to add bright details and brush textures. By Laurel Loomis, 1989. Courtesy of the artist.

A Gallery of Mixed Media Ideas

Watercolor is an especially effective medium for adding color to drawings done with oil pastels, crayons or markers.

By mixing more pigment into a watercolor wash, it is easy to create vibrant colors. Laura MacDonald, grade 8.

Washes may be cut up and used to create colorful fish, birds or butterflies. They stand out clearly when pasted to gray or blue paper. Danny Blank, grade 2.

Children studying about life on the farm in the United States drew pictures to show daily scenes. A few painted accents are effective when adding watercolor to fineline drawing. Sarah Willey, grade 3.

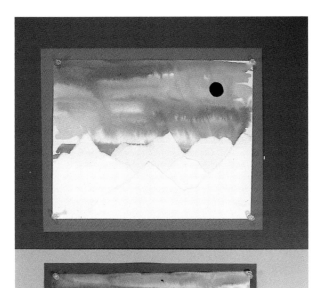

Students created washes of sunset skies. Then they tore large shapes from white paper and pasted them on top of these watercolor backgrounds. The torn edges suggested a snowy winter landscape of hills and mountains. Black silhouettes of trees, houses and animals cut from black construction paper were added. Using this technique, some classes made murals while others made individual greeting cards. Adele Adenio, art education student.

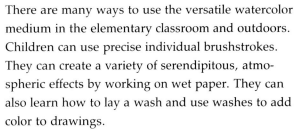

Summary

There are many ways to use the versatile watercolor medium in the elementary classroom and outdoors. Children can use precise individual brushstrokes. They can create a variety of serendipitous, atmospheric effects by working on wet paper. They can also learn how to lay a wash and use washes to add color to drawings.

Children especially enjoy working on a small scale and using their watercolor experiments as greeting cards, postcards and stationery.

Part Four
Thinking About the Painting Process

How do children know if they are done with a painting? How do they know whether or not they have succeeded? When a child completes an outstanding painting or creates a particularly beautiful effect in some part of a painting, it is important to acknowledge that achievement. When no feedback is given, children often come away unaware of their own accomplishments. As children grow in their ability to use an art vocabulary to analyze recognized works of art, they will also be better able to discuss their own artworks with one another and will do so if encouraged. The criteria you set beforehand give children a few guidelines against which they can measure their work. Their own sense of what is pleasing, which has been developing over time, gives them a few more clues. But in the end, children need, and have a right to expect, you to establish a laboratory atmosphere so they can evaluate their art experiences and resulting paintings.

Life in an elementary classroom during the usual forty-five minute or hour art period generates a particular kind of energy and rhythm. Since a major part of learning about art and the art process happens when teachers and children talk about art, evaluation and discussion should be an integral part of that rhythm. However, it is easy for both children and teachers to get caught up in the process and the mechanics of painting and cleanup. For that reason, it is helpful to plan for a short evaluation or discussion time during the art period.

Sara Curtain, grade 4.

Children who finish early can work on a group painting of the same lesson. Have a large piece of paper ready to set out on the floor or in the corner of a classroom. This allows children to build on the skills and concepts they have just been using. These children are eager to add their work to a group mural and to try using their skills to paint new animals and people.

13 Improving the Painting Process

Extending the Painting Process

Children work in different styles and at different rates. There are always children who work quickly and finish early. Since we want every part of the art process to be meaningful, it is necessary to keep in mind strategies for extending the painting process. The following are a few simple ways to enrich the painting experience for the child who finishes early.

• Step back to evaluate the completed painting with the child.

• Give out a small paintbrush and suggest that the child use it to add details.

• Encourage the child to choose a background color for mounting his or her painting.

• Hand out a smaller piece of paper, and encourage the child to do a painting of choice or another variation on the painting activity.

• Have index cards available so the child can write a title and name card for his or her painting.

• Set out a larger piece of paper, and ask the child to add to a group mural based on the same objectives as the lesson just completed.

• Give out oil pastels to add bright details. Encourage the child to press firmly and add light colors to dark areas or dark colors to light areas. Oil pastels may also be used to add texture.

Evaluation and Discussion

An evaluation at the elementary level does not mean criticism. Rather, it means looking at artwork with a critical eye. It means being able to identify what is working well and what needs improvement in any given work of art. It is important for all children to come away from evaluations feeling positive about some aspect of their paintings. For this reason, it is best to abide by the rule that comments about any work of art must be positive and helpful. Evaluations should also help children decide where to proceed from any given point. Evaluations may focus on the techniques, design, style of working or emotional impact of paintings.

Evaluations can take place during the motivation part of the lesson, during the work period or at

Looking at one's work on display and discussing the results with classmates and teacher are important parts of the art experience. Here, teacher and children are discussing the ways children painted water, sky and weather.

the end of the art class. They are probably most helpful when done while children are engaged in painting or just before they are about to add to paintings in progress, since evaluations tend to generate ideas. The evaluation time is an exciting, open time when children come to realize just what it is that is special about their paintings. It is a time to help children capitalize on the unique qualities of their work. It is also a time to make changes and reinforce skills and art concepts. It is a time to catch problems before it is too late to fix them. It is a time to comment on art as a process, a way of learning. Evaluations can also be times to take stock of just what the class as a whole has accomplished. It is a time to put the art activity into some kind of context.

Leading an Evaluation

Evaluations can be done individually, in small groups or with an entire class. They need not be long, formal or tedious. Often, a sentence or two will do. One of the easiest ways to help children

look at their work with objectivity is to ask them to stop, stand up and look at their paintings from a distance. Be sure to give them something to look for! For example: "Look to see whether you have included tiny, medium and very large shapes. Check to see whether you have repeated your colors. Have you used four different line textures? Check to see whether or not your animal stands out from the background. Look for something you did well in your painting or that your neighbor did in his or her painting; maybe it is the way you painted the scales on a fish or the way you mixed colors in your sky. Maybe it is an interesting texture you invented."

With a well-behaved class, you might encourage children to take a few minutes to walk around the room and look at the ways their classmates have solved a particular art problem. Again, children should look for specifics so that attention will be focused on unique solutions rather than on liking or disliking the paintings they see.

Sometimes a teacher wants to make a few points quickly without taking time for a discussion.

Making those points by using children's work as examples is an effective way to do this. You can ask children to stop their work and gather in the front of the room, or ask children to stop, put down their paintbrushes and give you their attention. Hold a few paintings up and make clear, specific comments: "I want you to notice that the artist of this painting placed one big animal in the foreground and several small animals high up in the background. This is a very good way to show distance in a painting. The artist of this picture used another technique to show distance in her painting. She used bright colors in the foreground, where objects are closer and clearer, and duller, softer colors in the distance, where objects are not as distinct. The artist of this picture tried something else. He made the road wide in the foreground and narrower and higher in the background to show that the road winds back into the distance. This artist used the same technique, but with fences instead of a road. When you go back to finish your painting, choose one technique to show distance in your painting."

When planning for an evaluation or discussion, limit the time to no more than five or ten minutes, especially for young children. Focus on one or two skills or concepts — ones students have understood and used well or ones that seem to be presenting problems. The way you phrase a question can make a big difference in the way children respond. Ask questions that call for specific responses. Children might be asked "What do you especially like about the way Alex used shape in his painting? What techniques did Jessica use to make the sky so dramatic in her painting? Who can tell me how Ben made his furry cat stand out from the shaggy rug?" Think through specific questions you will pose beforehand. Since it is difficult to talk about everyone's work, choose a few paintings to discuss. It is important, however, to include everyone's painting in an evaluation at one time or another. Therefore, you must keep track of who has not had a turn.

It is particularly important to be sensitive to a child who is having difficulty with a painting. Stress

Simply holding up paintings and pointing out what seems to be working well is one way to help children see their paintings with some objectivity. This child is showing his teacher how he created a feeling of movement in his ocean painting.

the positive — what the child is doing well: "I can see that you are really concentrating; you have included three different kinds of lines. You remembered to overlap." Using that child's painting as an example of one of the lesson objectives can also help build the child's confidence: "Sam has used five different values of gray in his weather painting. Notice how the brushstrokes of the clouds go in a different direction from the brushstrokes of the rain." By pointing out what is working well, teachers help children see their work in a positive light. Usually a child whose painting has been used as an example will feel renewed interest in his or her work and will return to painting with a different attitude.

Discussion Topics

The following topics are suggestions for focusing discussions. Don't try to talk about too many aspects of the art process at once or children will be overwhelmed and start to lose interest. It is helpful to be clear on one or two main points so the discussion remains short and specific. Usually the nature of the lesson itself or problems and discoveries that come up while children are working generate the agenda for a discussion. One of the most creative parts of teaching is choosing which aspect of the art experience to highlight and how to make it exciting and applicable to children's lives.

Which art elements did the artist emphasize in this painting? Is the painting basically linear? Was the artist especially interested in exploring some aspect of color — light colors, earth tones, contrasting colors, different values of gray? How would you describe the shapes in this painting? Are they curvy or straight-edged, hard-edged or soft-edged? Is it the textures in the painting that seem most immediate?

How is this painting organized? Where is the center of interest? Why do you think the artist placed it there? What devices did the artist use to make it stand out? How does your eye move through this painting? Are certain colors, lines, shapes or patterns repeated? Is there a particular

direction or kind of movement in the painting? Did the artist achieve balance in a formal or informal way?

What is the subject of this painting? Is this a realistic painting, a nonobjective painting or an abstract painting? Is this a still life, landscape, cityscape, oceanscape, cloudscape or portrait? What aspect of the subject was the artist particularly interested in showing? Do you think the artist was especially interested in design, in imitating something from the real world or in evoking an emotional response?

How would you describe the painting style of this artist? Does the painting seem finished? Is the whole paper covered with paint? How did the artist achieve variety? Unity? What special techniques did the artist use — dry brush, painting on wet paper, textural? Would you describe the style as bold, free, strong, delicate, precise, detailed, somber?

What message do you think the artist is trying to give in this painting? Does this painting tell something about the way people or animals live or act? Does it tell about a specific place or part of the country or world? Does it show the world from a particularly unusual perspective or at a specific time of day? Does this painting cause you to think about something in a new way?

What effect does this painting have on you? How does it make you feel? Scared? Happy? Angry? Quiet? Can you associate this painting with an emotion such as love, joy, delight, fear, pain, sorrow?

The artist wanted to capture the spiritual essence of the Taos Pueblo. Ask students, "What is a pueblo? What do you think the artist means by 'the spiritual essence'? What kind of shapes and colors did she use to make this painting feel magical?" Katalin Ehling, *Magical Afternoon*. Watercolor, 52" x 40" (132 cm x 102 cm). Courtesy of the artist and the Suzanne Brown Gallery.

Matting and Displaying Paintings

Displays can be powerful teaching and learning tools. Mounting and displaying children's artwork is a way of celebrating and calling attention to their achievements. Displays give students a chance to see their work at its best. They give students a chance to step back and see their work with more objectivity and in comparison to work of other students. Displays also give children an opportunity to give and receive positive feedback from other children, teachers and parents. Displays present another opportunity for talking about, and evaluating, works of art.

What Makes an Effective Display?

Each piece of artwork to be displayed should be shown to its best advantage. In planning displays, it is best to include everyone's effort. If that is not possible, be sure to keep track of whose work you have displayed so each child has a turn eventually. Consider which students would benefit most by having their work on display. Putting a child's work on display is a way of complimenting that child. It can boost a child's confidence. Keep in mind that displays can be changed frequently. After a week or so, they tend to become part of the walls.

Matting a painting is easy to do, and it makes a big difference in giving a painting a finished look. A valuable trick is to trim an inch or more from the length and width of standard-size sheets of paper before handing them to children for a painting lesson. Once paintings have dried, they are easy to position and mount on standard-size sheets of construction paper. They don't have to be cut down to fit mats. Rather than trimming the edges of one painting at a time so it will fit on a large sheet of paper, this simple solution can save many, many hours. It also saves paper.

As a general rule, choose a color that has been used in the painting itself for the mat. This is an effective way of enhancing the finished painting. A

Children are intrigued to see that the color of the mat can change the effect of their painting. Choosing a background color is a way to help them become sensitive to this phenomenon.

As a general rule, tell children to select a background color from one of the colors in their painting. This painting was an exercise in mixing tints. Simone Topal, age 8.

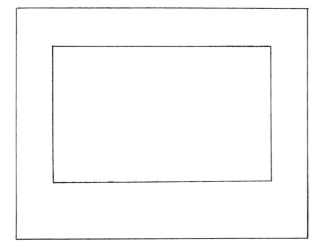

mat that repeats a color from the painting also unifies the painting. For children who finish their paintings early, choosing a mat color and mounting a painting can be an intriguing experience. Lay out or hang a few different background colors. Children can try their paintings against each color to see which background is most effective. They can witness firsthand what a big difference an effective background color can make. Sometimes you will want to choose one color on which to mount all the paintings. This can help give the display as a whole more impact.

When mounting a display, it is helpful to keep in mind that a display is actually a large composition. The same principles that apply to composing an individual work of art — repetition, rhythm, balance, contrast, emphasis, variety, movement — also apply to composing a display. Using larger sheets of construction paper behind a few paintings is an easy way to highlight a small grouping. When beginning a display, tack the pictures only at the top to get an idea about spacing. You will probably have to move pictures around several times before actually tacking down all four corners. Use the edges of walls, bulletin boards and of other pictures as guidelines to help hang the picture straight. Consider hanging your displays at the eye level of students, if they are the intended viewers. Higher displays are more appropriate for adult viewers. Key words and explanations give viewers clues to what they should be looking for. "Paintings to Music" is an example of a title. "Students listened for staccato and legato sounds, high and low sounds and fast and slow sounds" is an example of a more directed explanation that mentions skills and concepts.

When a painting is tacked to a wall or bulletin board, it seems to assume visual weight. If a painting were mounted so that each side of the border were equal, its visual weight would make the border on the bottom appear smaller. To counteract this effect, the dimension of the margin at the bottom must be slightly wider than the margins at the sides and top. After positioning the paper correctly, tape or staple it to the paper mat.

Thinking up a title and writing it on a small card is an excellent way to extend and enrich the painting process. Thinking up a title means stepping back to take another look at one's work and perhaps discussing it with a classmate or the teacher. *The Mad Scientist,* Rachel Topal, grade 3.

Sometimes children enjoy creating their own frames. For this project, ornate frames were made by squeezing glue onto a piece of cardboard to make a raised design. After the glue dried, gold acrylic was painted over the cardboard. Colonial portrait, Katherine Barnes, grade 5.

Displays are a way to help parents understand what their children are working on in the classroom. A display of cubist portraits by sixth-graders.

Signing the Painting

Each piece of a student's artwork should be signed, or you can write the name of the child on a card. To keep track of who did what painting, it is wise to get children in the habit of writing their names on the backs of papers before beginning to paint. Another way to record names is to write each child's name lightly in pencil at the top or the bottom of the painting while children are working. This is a great way to be sure you have checked in with each child during the course of an art lesson.

It makes sense to teach children to pay attention to the way they sign their paintings. Warn children not to let their signatures dominate or take away from the rest of their paintings. Signatures should not be overly large. Warn children to avoid placing their signatures directly in the middle of artworks. Usually paintings are signed in the bottom right-hand corner. It is fun to point out signatures when looking at works of art by outstanding artists. Parallelling a line or shape at the bottom of the painting when placing one's signature can be effective.

On some paintings, artists have included the date and year of completion. That is certainly helpful information for art historians to have when they are trying to figure out in what order and during what time period a particular painting was created. You may wish to have children date their work.

Titles are not usually written directly on paintings; they are usually mounted on plaques or cards next to, or at the bottom of, paintings. Names and titles should be neatly written on small white cards with a black marker.

When painting a picture of himself, Rivera painted a piece of paper with an inscription, the date and his name. Direct students to sign their paintings by placing their signatures in such a way that they become part of the compositions, or to just place them in the bottom corners so that they do not take away from the paintings. Diego Rivera, *Self-Portrait*, 1941. Oil on canvas, 23″ x 16⅞″ (61 cm x 43 cm). Smith College Museum of Art, Northampton, Massachusetts.

Alison Davis Wade, grade 2.

Summary

Evaluations, discussions and displays are all ways to encourage children to look at and think about the art process and the results of the art experience. They are ways of helping children see their own work within the larger framework of human experience. They are ways of helping children understand that their artworks are part of the visual tradition of people reacting to the times and circumstances in which they live.

It is easy and efficient to use baby food jars filled with different colors of paint. Before children begin painting, remind them to watch where they place their jars of paint. Jars placed at the edge of the work surface topple easily. It is better to hold the jar with one hand or place it in the middle of the table. Also remind children to take care when reaching for a new color. It is easy to knock down a container with a paintbrush sticking out of it.

When using baby food jars as containers, try to collect jars of the same size. This makes it easy to stack whole trays of paint for storage.

Children can select colors and brushes from this cart to use at the easel. Only a few children will be painting at a time at the easels in the background.

14 Painting Supplies

There is nothing as enticing to children as freshly prepared colors of gleaming paint awaiting their use! It is a teacher's job to assemble the necessary materials and think through the paint distribution system that best suits the circumstances. Some teachers who feel that children should learn how to prepare their own paints develop systems to facilitate paint preparation as an activity. Trying out the painting activity and the paint distribution system beforehand is one way to spot potential problems. Painting activities can be carried out with surprisingly little mess if the teacher is prepared.

Any waterbase paint works well in the elementary classroom. New painting supplies designed for the classroom continue to be developed and perfected. The following are descriptions of basic paint supply options. Supplies for black ink painting and watercolor painting are listed separately in Chapters 11 and 12.

Tempera Paint

Thick, creamy tempera paint is the traditional painting medium for the elementary classroom. Though some teachers prefer to mix their own tempera paint from powder, liquid tempera is generally quicker, safer and easier to use, and it comes in the proper pea-soup consistency. If the paint seems too thick, a little water can be mixed in. Liquid tempera is an ideal medium for children. It is expressive, immediate and bold, and colors can be mixed easily. Liquid tempera is packaged in a wide range of colors and sizes. Standard colors include black, white, blue, brown, green, orange, yellow, red, violet, magenta, peach and turquoise. Silver, gold and fluorescent colors of tempera paint are also available for special effects. When ordering colors, it is important to realize that the light colors — yellow and white — get used up first, so double up on the amount of those.

Tempera paint works well on almost any surface. White 60 lb. (or heavier) vellum paper is the most popular painting surface. Tempera paint also

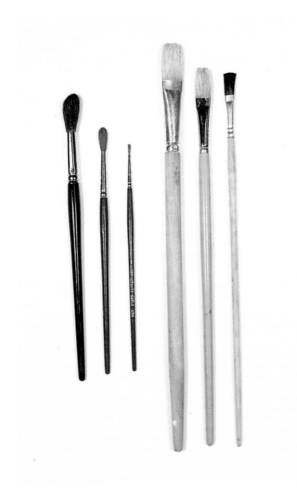

Flat, stiff easel brushes of a variety of sizes, and small, medium and large watercolor brushes work well for most painting projects.

works well on manila, bogus and construction papers as well as on cardboard, wood or mural paper because all the surfaces are absorbent.

A flat, stiff, good quality ⅜″ easel brush can be used for most painting projects. It can cover wide areas easily, yet it is narrow enough to use for brush drawing and painting in smaller details. It is always helpful to have the option of a stiff ¼″ easel brush for smaller details and a ¾″ or 1″ brush for murals. Small, medium and large watercolor brushes can also be used with tempera paint. The soft bristles and points allow for more expressivity when children have developed some control over

the brushes. Over time, it is helpful for children to have experienced several different kinds and sizes of brushes. As children develop skill in painting, they will want to choose the kinds of brushes they use for particular paintings.

Distributing Tempera Paint

Teachers use a variety of systems for presenting and distributing tempera paint to children. Each system depends on the ages of the children and the classroom situation. For younger elementary children, baby food jars with lids are popular containers for storing paint. They are easy to obtain, they fit into the shelves of most easels, the color of the paint shows through the glass, they seem to hold just the right amount of paint and they are just the right height and weight for holding brushes.

When painting with a whole class of younger elementary children at once, it is convenient to use a system in which each child needs only one jar of paint and one brush at a time. When children are ready to change colors, the brush goes back into the jar and both jar and brush are placed back on a central tray or passed to another child. Colors stay relatively pure with this system, and very little paint is wasted with brush washing. No water is necessary, only jars of paint, so distribution and cleanup are accomplished easily. This system of painting has the advantage of fostering extremely bright, colorful and unified paintings — especially if tints and a variety of mixed colors are included in the paint selections.

The length of the paintbrush can make a big difference with this system. Brushes with shorter handles help eliminate the spilling that can occur with longer easel brushes. Sometimes teachers choose to use number 12 watercolor brushes because the handles are two inches shorter than standard easel brushes.

When a teacher wants to make a variety of colors available to children at the same time, plastic ice cube trays, muffin tins or Styrofoam egg con-

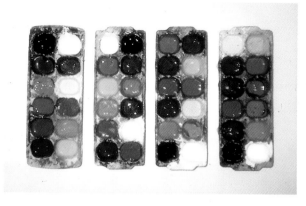

Plastic ice cube trays work well when you wish to make all colors available at once. These trays hold enough paint for several children to work from one tray.

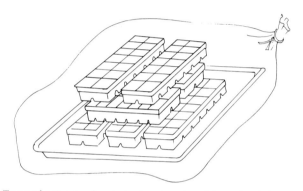

Trays of paint can be stacked and enclosed in a plastic bag for storage at the end of the day.

tainers are useful since they have the right amount of spaces. Plastic ice cube trays hold up very well over the years. To store paint overnight, a coating of water can be placed over each color. A quick stir returns the paint to the right consistency. At the end of a painting unit, trays can be allowed to dry out, and the dry cakes of tempera can be popped out and thrown away. Dried trays of tempera paint can also be saved and reused. Adding water a day or two before you wish to use them allows water to sink down and moisten the caked tempera. Stir up each color before distributing to children.

Some teachers feel strongly that children should have their own trays with the primary colors plus black and white. When using this system, children can develop an excellent sense of how to mix and control colors. Glass or plastic furniture casters or jar lids half filled with paint would be arranged in a specific order with light colors closest to the child and darker colors farthest away. A row of casters would contain white, yellow, red, blue and black, in that order. A water container and sponge for wiping the brush would also be included in each tray. Trays for right-handed children should be placed to the children's right; trays for left-handed children should be arranged on the opposite side. Trays can be stacked and covered with a large plastic bag at the end of the day.

Learning to Use Tempera Paint

Review basic ways to use tempera paints and brushes each year. In general, it is important to wet easel brushes and wipe them on dry paper towels or sponges before inserting them into easel paint. A premoistened, but not dripping wet, brush picks up

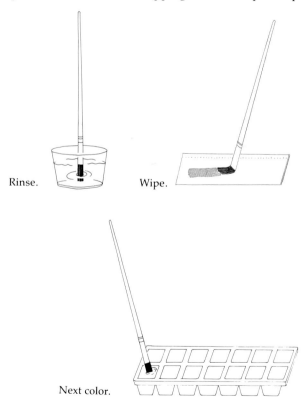

Rinse.

Wipe.

Next color.

just the right amount of paint, whereas a dry brush tends to pick up a large glob. Stir the paint. Wipe the brush on the edge of the jar or container of paint before using it in order to remove excess paint. Be sure to return the brush to the same color jar if you are using the jar system. If you are changing colors, wash the brush by gently stirring it in the bottom of the water container and wiping it on a sponge or paper towel to remove excess water and pigment.

Opaque Tempera Blocks

Tempera blocks are cakes of highly concentrated pigment that mix easily with water. They are especially handy when traveling among classrooms. Tempera blocks come in sets of basic colors, so virtually no paint preparation is involved. Individual cakes are also sold separately as replacements, but you can always add a squeeze of liquid tempera if a color runs out. Be sure that white is one of the colors available in the paint sets, if you choose this system. Children especially enjoy mixing tints with white paint.

Tempera blocks don't usually have the rich, creamy consistency of liquid tempera paints unless the child spends time working the pigment and water together. Dried tempera cakes provide a different experience. They work especially well for detailed paintings because children are able to control the consistency fairly easily. They work well in regular classroom settings because they are less messy to deal with.

Tempera blocks yield light colors when mixed with a lot of water, as well as denser, deeper colors as more pigment is mixed in. Tempera blocks work especially well when painting clay, wooden or cardboard sculptures.

Tempera cakes come in large and small containers. Teach children to place a few drops of water on each dry cake before beginning to paint. Using the brush in one direction, they should work the pigment and water together to achieve a deep, vibrant color. Remind students to keep adding water and working it into the pigment while painting; this is a technique that needs to be reviewed. Often children do not think to do this. Instead, they scrub hard with their brushes.

Acrylic Paint

Upper elementary children enjoy trying new kinds of paint. Recently several manufacturers have come out with affordable, washable acrylic paints for the school classroom. Acrylic paints have the wonderful creamy consistency of tempera paints yet are easier to manipulate. Acrylics have the transluscency of watercolor paints when used with a lot of water. They can also create the thick, textured effects of oil paints. Acrylics come in tubes or jars and should be squeezed or poured each day because they are quick-drying. Sometimes, palettes of specially mixed colors can be saved by being covered with plastic wrap overnight.

Special brushes designed for use with acrylic paints are affordably priced. Other brushes may also be used. It is important to remember that acrylic paints are washable when wet, but are permanent when dry. Brushes need to be washed right away after painting with acrylics.

Acrylic paints may be used on any paper surface. It is also a unique experience for children to paint on sheets of canvas, canvas board or Canvasette paper that are made specifically for acrylic paints. Pads of disposable paper palettes are convenient for mixing. Using professional materials makes the experience of painting with acrylics a very special one for beginners.

Additional Supplies

A collection of water dishes of the same size is important to have on hand. Plastic containers from sherbet, yogurt, cottage cheese or take-out foods work well and can be stacked for storage. Fill them half full to eliminate spills. When there is no sink in the classroom, a bucket of water is a good substitute. An extra bucket is helpful for collecting dirty water.

Flat Styrofoam trays or disposable pie tins come in handy for mixing colors. They are much easier to clean than plastic palettes with indentations, and there is much less wasted paint when using flat mixing surfaces. Collecting trays of the same size simplifies storage.

Newspapers or other kinds of table coverings are a must when using any kind of paint.

Disposable coated paper cups are another handy option for distributing paint. They are especially convenient when a teacher begins a class with one or two colors and then wishes to make additional colors available. Covering cups of paints with a large plastic bag will keep them moist for several days.

Plastic tubs used for washing dishes are excellent containers for transporting an entire classroom set of watercolors or tempera blocks as well as for storing supplies. Plastic trays are handy for storing and transporting jars of paint to and from a table.

Empty vegetable, juice or coffee cans can become storage containers for brushes. Be sure to rinse brushes well in cool or lukewarm water and store them with the bristles pointed up. Don't use hot water because it can melt the glue that attaches the bristles to the ferrules.

A good supply of paper towels is helpful for wiping brushes before changing colors; paper towels

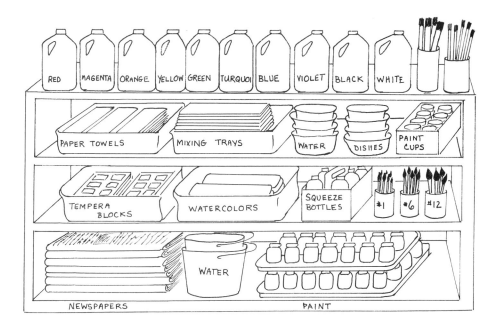

Take time to organize supplies. When supplies are labeled and kept in containers, they are easy to find, transport, clean up and put away.

are more absorbent than newspaper. Absorbent cellulose sponges are another alternative for soaking up excess water.

When using liquid tempera paints, it is helpful to have squeeze bottles of each color to use in a pinch to refill children's paint trays during class.

A space for drying wet paintings is especially important when painting with a whole class or when several classes in a row come to paint. Several kinds of drying racks are available commercially. Many teachers set up clothes racks or hang cords and use clothespins to hold paintings as they dry. Completed paintings can also be placed on the floor in a specific section of the room until they are dry.

Smocks are necessary for painting. Extra-large T-shirts make good smocks and can be slipped on and off quickly. Large "Daddy" or "Mommy" shirts with the sleeves cropped can be buttoned down the back. Children can help button one another.

Setting Up and Cleaning Up

Setting up a classroom for painting is not difficult and takes only a few minutes if paints are prepared beforehand. Simply cover tables with newspapers, and place a piece of paper, a paper towel and a brush at each place. Then put out enough paint sets and water dishes so each child has easy access to the supplies.

If children do their own setting up, it is helpful to have all supplies available in one place. That way, children can first cover their work areas with newspapers and then go get their supplies. When finished, supplies can be returned to the distribution area and brushes and water dishes placed in the sink for one or two children to wash. When children are responsible for setting up and cleaning up, they become more independent in their work habits and they also learn proper care for art materials.

Ideally, children can learn to position their painting colors next to the hands they use for painting. This isn't always possible when children share

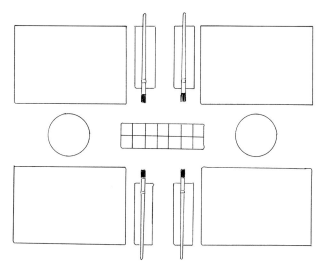

A table set up for four children to paint.

trays of paints, and most often this is not a problem. However, if a child is having trouble manipulating the paint, look at which hand the child is using and try to move the paint and water dish nearer to that hand. Repositioning the child is another way to help. Having a few extra trays of paint to give to individual children can be helpful, too.

Summary

You and your students will feel calmer, and the art class will proceed more smoothly, if you have developed systems for distributing and storing painting supplies and organizing clean-up. An effective organization enables children to be more independent. They can find what they need, use it, clean it and return it to its proper storage place. This leaves you free to interact with individual children.

Preparing for and organizing the movement of supplies, children and wet paintings within a particular classroom setting is an art in itself. Time spent thinking through procedures and collecting necessary materials will prove itself to be an excellent investment again and again, throughout the year.

Glossary

abstract A form that has been simplified or geometricized.

acrylic A plastic painting medium that can be used like watercolor or oil paints; a water-based paint that becomes permanent when dry.

art elements The visual "tools" artists use to create art, including line, shape, color, texture, value and space.

background The part of a painting that appears to be farthest away from the viewer.

balance The equilibrium of various elements in a work of art.

blob method A technique of creating forms in a painting by using a brush to push out a mass of paint.

bogus paper A gray, dual-textured heavyweight paper, commonly used for tempera painting. It is rough on one side, smooth on the other.

center of interest The part of a work of art that first draws the viewer's attention.

cityscape A work of art in which the city is the predominant subject.

cloudscape A work of art in which clouds predominate.

color family A grouping of hues that are based on one color, such as green. Yellow-green, grass-green, light green, army green and blue-green are examples of colors in the green color family.

composition The arrangement of art elements in a work of art.

contrasting colors Hues that are opposite one another on the color wheel.

cool colors Blue, green and violet, as well as colors containing a predominant amount of blue, green or violet.

earth tones A family of colors also known as neutral colors; those pigments made from natural minerals or different colors of earth.

expressionism A painting style in which the artist uses strong colors and brushstrokes to communicate emotional responses to a particular subject matter.

Fauvism A style of painting in France in the early twentieth century. These painters were nicknamed "Fauves," meaning "wild beasts," because of their use of bright and intense colors to express emotion.

ferrule The metal part of a brush that holds the bristles to the handle.

foreground The part of a painting that appears to be closest to the viewer.

formal balance A symmetrical composition.

freeform Irregular shapes or forms; shapes or forms that are not geometric.

geometric Shapes or forms that are regular and precise; shapes or forms that are based on geometric structures — squares, circles, triangles, rectangles, cones, cubes, spheres, pyramids, cylinders, etc.

harmonious colors Colors that look pleasing together; hues that are near one another on the color wheel. Red-orange, red and violet are a set of harmonious colors. A color family is composed of harmonious colors.

horizon line The place where the earth meets the sky.

Impressionism An art movement in which painters attempted to capture candid glimpses of their subjects through spontaneous brushwork and an emphasis on the momentary effects of sunlight on color. These artists aimed at achieving an impression of reality, rather than a photographic representation of their subjects.

informal balance A type of visual balance in which the two sides of a composition are different but balanced; asymmetrical balance. Informal balance is achieved by adjusting the visual weight of the art elements.

intermediate colors Colors made by mixing a primary hue with a secondary hue; also called tertiary colors. Yellow-orange, red-violet and blue-green are examples of intermediate hues.

landscape A work of art in which the features of the land (desert, mountains, trees, forest) are the predominant subject.

linear Having to do with lines; a painting technique in which line stands out as the predominant art element.

manila paper A buff colored paper, especially useful for paintings in which the whole paper surface is meant to be covered with tempera paint.

mark A brushstroke.

middleground The part of a painting that lies between the background and the foreground.

monochromatic A work of art that uses variations of a single color.

mural A very large painting, often painted by several people.

negative space The parts of a painting that are not filled with subject matter, but are still part of the overall composition.

neutral colors When all three primary colors are mixed together, or when pairs of contrasting colors are mixed together, they yield a neutral gray or brown color. When white or black is added to any of these mixtures, other lighter or darker neutral colors such as beige and dark gray are created.

nonobjective Art with no recognizable subject matter; non-representational art.

opaque Not allowing light to pass through; a paint that is not transparent.

open-ended An art problem that has many different solutions; an art problem that each child can solve in his or her own special way.

optical color mixing A phenomenon that occurs when small strokes of contrasting colors are placed in close proximity to one another. The eye tends to see the color area as a mixture of the two different colors.

overpainting Painting on top of a dry painted surface.

organic Shapes or forms that are irregular, usually curvilinear, and suggestive of shapes or forms found in nature.

organizing principles Concepts that help artists think about how to arrange the art elements in a work of art, including balance, movement, variety, repetition, emphasis, rhythm, contrast and unity.

painterly Used to describe a painting in which the brushstrokes are evident.

palette A surface used for mixing colors; also refers to the colors that an artist has chosen to use in a particular painting.

pattern A design made by repeating a motif at regular intervals.

picture plane The entire painting surface.

pigment A coloring matter, often powder, that is mixed with water, oil or another binder to make paint.

point of view The angle from which the viewer sees an object or scene. An artist may select to paint an object from a front, back, side, top (bird's eye), bottom or three-quarter point of view.

Pointillism A style of painting developed in France in the nineteenth century in which paint is applied to canvas in small dots of color.

portrait A painting of a particular person.

primary colors The hues from which all other colors on the color wheel can be made: red, yellow and blue.

radial symmetry Spreading or branching out in all directions from a common center.

rhythm The visual flow throughout a painting; the way one's eyes read or move through a work of art. The repetition of a shape, line or color can create a sense of rhythm in a painting.

roughing in the shapes Lightly sketching the main large shapes in a composition to plan how they will fit onto the paper.

secondary colors Hues made by mixing equal amounts of two primary colors: orange, green and violet.

serendipitous painting A painting in which the results happen spontaneously.

shade Any dark value of a color, usually achieved by adding black.

silhouette An outline drawing filled in with a single color; any dark shape or outline seen against a light background.

sketch In painting, a planning drawing done with a wash of paint as a preliminary layout of the main shapes in a composition.

skill A developed proficiency in creating a desired effect.

skyline The outline of a city as seen against the sky.

skyscape A work of art in which the sky is the predominant subject.

still life An arrangement of inanimate objects as a subject for painting or drawing.

strong lines The structural lines that seem to break up the picture plane in a composition.

style The distinctive features that characterize the way an artist works.

sumi-e Japanese brush ink painting.

symmetry The placement of the same elements on either side of a dividing line in such a way that they form a mirror image of each other; this arrangement results in formal or symmetrical balance.

texture The quality of a surface, usually characterized by its roughness or smoothness. Texture can refer to both the visual and tactile quality of a surface.

textural A painting in which texture is the predominating art element.

tint Any light value of a color, usually achieved by adding white.

tone A color that is dulled or "toned down" through the addition of black and white (gray).

tooth The textured surface of paper which holds or grips paint in unique ways.

transparent A paint that can be seen through; opposite of opaque.

value The lightness or darkness of a color.

viewpoint The angle from which the viewer sees an object or scene; the position of the artist when creating a work of art.

warm colors Yellow, orange and red, as well as colors containing a predominant amount of yellow, orange or red.

waterscape (oceanscape, seascape) A work of art in which a body of water is the predominant subject.

wash A thin or watery coating of paint.

watercolor Transparent or semi-transparent water-soluble paint.

Bibliography

Some of the following books are no longer in print, but may be available at your local library.

Barber, Richard and Anne Riches, *A Dictionary of Fabulous Beasts.* New York: Macmillan, Inc., 1971.

Barnett, Vivian E., *Kandinsky: At the Guggenheim Museum.* New York: Abbeville Press, Inc., 1983.

Brommer, Gerald and Nancy Kinne, *Exploring Painting.* Worcester, MA: Davis Publications, Inc., 1988.

Brookes, Mona, *Drawing With Children: A Creative Teaching & Learning Method That Works For Adults, Too.* Los Angeles: Jeremy P. Tarcher Inc., 1986.

Chapman, Laura H., *Discover Art,* (grades 1–6). Worcester, MA: Davis Publications, Inc., 1985.

Chieh Tzu Yuan Hua Chuan, 1679–1701, *The Mustard Seed Garden Manual of Painting:* A Facsimile of the 1887–1888 Shanghai edition. Translated and edited by Mai-Mai Sze. Princeton, NJ: Princeton University Press, 1956.

Cole, Natalie Robinson, *The Arts in the Classroom.* The John Day Co., 1940.

Davis, Marilyn Kornreich in collaboration with Arnold Broido, *Music Dictionary.* Garden City, NY: Doubleday and Co., Inc., 1956.

Day, Michael and Al Hurwitz, *Children and Their Art,* 5th ed. Orlando, FL: Harcourt Brace Jovanovich, Inc., 1991.

de Paola, Tomie, *The Cloud Book.* New York: Scholastic, Inc., 1975.

Evans, Jane, *Chinese Brush Painting.* New York: Watson-Guptill Publications, 1987.

Gatto, Joseph, Albert W. Porter, and Jack Selleck, *Exploring Visual Design.* Worcester, MA: Davis Publications, Inc., 1978.

Herberholz, Barbara and Lee Hanson, *Early Childhood Art.* Dubuque, IA: Wm. C. Brown Publishers, 1985.

Hollingsworth, Patricia L., "Apples and Onions: Art Categories, Criticism and Appreciation." *School Arts,* April 1987.

Kellogg, Rhoda, *Analyzing Children's Art.* Palo Alto, CA: Mayfield Publishing Company, 1970.

Lansing, Kenneth and Arlene Richards, *Elementary Teacher's Art Handbook.* Orlando, FL: Holt, Rinehart & Winston, Inc., 1981.

Parramón, M. and G. Fresquet, *How to Paint in Watercolor.* New York: Watson-Guptill Publications, 1988.

Read, Herbert, *A Concise History of Modern Painting.* New York: Oxford University Press, 1974.

Schmalz, Carl, *Watercolor Your Way.* New York: Watson-Guptill Publications, Inc., 1978.

Siudzinski, Paul, *Japanese Brush Painting Techniques, Sumi-e, A Meditation in Ink.* New York: Sterling Publishing Co., Inc., 1978.

Smith, Nancy R., *Experience and Art, Teaching Children to Paint.* New York: Teachers College Press, 1983.

Szekely, George, "Conversations in the Art Class," *Art Education,* May 1982, pp. 15–17.

Wachowiak, Frank, *Emphasis Art: A Qualitative Art Program for Elementary and Middle Schools.* 4th ed., New York: Harper & Row, 1985.

White, T.H., *The Book of Beasts.* Mineala, NY: Dover Publications, Inc., 1984.

Wilson, Marjorie and Brent Wilson, *Teaching Children to Draw: A Guide For Teachers and Parents.* Englewood Cliffs, NJ: Prentice-Hall, Inc., 1982.

Yamada, Sadami, *Complete Sumi-e Techniques.* San Francisco, CA: Japan Publications Trading Co., 1966.

Index